LZ

COWBOY

A Cowboy's Journal
1979–1981

LZ
COWBOY

A Cowboy's Journal
1979–1981

By
John R. Erickson

Photographs By Kris Erickson

University of North Texas Press
Denton Texas

5 4 3 2 1

Permissions
University of North Texas Press
P. O. Box 13856
Denton, Texas 76203-6856

The paper in this book meets the minimum requirements of the
American National Standard for Permanence of Paper for Printed
Library Materials, Z39.48-1984.

Number Three: Western Life Series

Library of Congress Cataloging-in-Publication Data
Erickson, John R., 1943–
LZ cowboy : a cowboy's journal, 1979–1981 / by John R. Erickson ;
photographs by Kris Erickson.
p.   cm — (Western life series ; 3)
Includes index.
ISBN 1-57441-024-5 (alk. paper)
1. Erickson, John R., 1943– —Diaries. 2. Cowboys—Texas—
Texas Panhandle—Diaries. 3. Texas Panhandle (Tex.)—Social life
and customs.   I. Title. II. Series.
F392.P168E75   1997
976.4'8063'092—dc21
[B]   96-40038
CIP
Cover design, Amy Layton
Cover photo, Kris Erickson
Interior design, Accent Design & Communications

Foreword

In the summer of 1979 I learned that Lawrence Ellzey was looking for a ranch hand. Lawrence and his son Tom had a cow/calf and yearling operation headquartered on Wolf Creek, some twenty-five miles southeast of Perryton, Texas, and I was interested in the job.

I had spent the past year and a half working one of the Barby ranches in Beaver County, Oklahoma. My time on the Beaver River had been very productive. Not only had I gotten a thorough education in the cowboy profession, but I had also managed to write *Panhandle Cowboy, The Modern Cowboy, Alkali County Tales*, and a number of articles in my small office in John Little's barn.

The move to Perryton and to the LZ Ranch appealed to me for several reasons. I wanted to be closer to my father who lived in Perryton. Also, though Perryton was hardly at the crossroads of the world, it was two hours closer to a major airport than our trailer house on the Beaver River. By 1979 my desire to become a professional writer required that

I make occasional trips out into the modern world, and access to the airport was important.

And then there was the appeal of working with the Ellzey family. I had known these people all my life. Some of my earliest memories included Lawrence playing the guitar and singing cowboy songs with his magnificent baritone voice; riding horses at the ranch; playing childhood games with the Ellzey boys; and Sunday lunch get-togethers at one family's house or the other.

In high school I played football and sang in the choir with John and Tom. At the University of Texas I shared a house with John and Lawrence, Jr., and sang in the UT a cappella choir with Tom and John. In the early 1970s, when Tom, John, and I ended up back in Perryton and started our own families, I worked cattle with the Ellzeys on my days off. Kris and I sang in Lawrence's choir at the First United Methodist Church, and then sang in the community's annual presentation of Handel's *Messiah*, which Lawrence started in the early 1950s and directed for some thirty years.

After Kris and I moved to the Crown Ranch in Beaver County in 1974, we continued to maintain our ties with the Ellzeys. We seldom missed the big Fourth of July picnic at the ranch, an annual affair begun by Lawrence's father, Thomas Virgil Ellzey, back in 1939. While I was managing the Crown Ranch (1974–78), I swapped out ranch work with John and Tom. I rode in their roundups and they came to mine. They always came well mounted and they always made good hands.

There were many qualities I admired in the Ellzey family, but the one which bound us most closely together was our love of ranch life, in all its forms and expressions: the beauty of a sunset on Wolf Creek; the changes in the weather; pride in horses and horsemanship; an endless curiosity about the land and the peculiar habits of animals; and most of all, the work.

Ranching is a hard life and a tough business, and anyone who doesn't have an appetite for hard work won't last long. The Ellzeys worked hard—all of them: men and women, young and old, brothers and sisters, husbands and wives, grandparents and grandchildren, uncles and aunts and cousins. They took pride in their work and they found ways of enjoying it. Work was what they did most and best, and I liked that.

The LZ Ranch was established in 1917 by Lawrence's father and his uncle Frank Ellzey. Frank was killed a year later when he roped a horse and was pulled into a tree. The ranch was located near the head of Wolf Creek, a tributary of the North Canadian River which flowed year-round, on land that had once been part of the sprawling Bar CC Ranch. After taking a degree in business from SMU in 1937, Lawrence moved back to the Panhandle with his bride, Mary Frances, and began ranching in partnership with his father. There, in the Wolf Creek Valley, they made their home and raised four sons and a daughter.

In 1979, when I joined the outfit, the LZ consisted of three parts: the "Upper Place," six sections of land with a house where Tom and Janet Ellzey lived; the "Lower Place," three sections with a house occupied during the summer by Lawrence and Mary Frances; and the "Dutcher Place," three sections of leased land that connected the two Ellzey places.

The Upper Place served as our headquarters, and it was to headquarters that I reported for work every morning. That's where we parked our vehicles and stock trailers, and where we kept our horses and saddles.

In August of 1979 Kris and I moved our kids and belongings to a little house in Perryton. It turned out to be the most difficult move we ever made. Two weeks beforehand, I had injured my back in a roping accident. I was out doctoring calves and was in hot pursuit of a small calf that had pinkeye. Just as I was about to make my throw, the calf cut sharply to the right. The horse I was riding, a sorrel Quarter Horse named Little John, was a pretty good cutting horse. He was quick and had good action. When he ducked right to follow the calf, I was standing up in my stirrups, swinging my rope.

That was the wrong place to be. I got caught off balance and came close to flying out of the saddle, which was something I didn't care to do. My right thigh caught the swell of my old Heiser saddle and kept me from taking a nasty fall, but the effort of staying in the saddle ripped all the muscles in my lower back. I knew I was hurt, though I didn't know how badly until later. I coiled up my rope, loaded Little John in the stock trailer, and drove eight miles back to headquarters on the river. By the time I got there, I could hardly walk and couldn't carry my saddle into the saddle shed. I left it on the ground, turned out Little John without any grain, and hobbled to the trailer house where we lived.

It was the worst injury I ever sustained in eight years of full-time cowboy work. I spent a week in bed and had to crawl on my hands and knees to the bathroom. The first night, when the big muscles in my lower back began to cramp, I wasn't sure I could stand the pain. If we hadn't lived thirty miles from town, I would have told Kris to call an ambulance. I was crippled up for six weeks. When we moved to Perryton, Kris had to do all the packing and loading by herself, for which she should receive the Pioneer Mother Award. When I went to work for the Ellzeys, I spent the first month or two in a back brace.

One result of this experience was that I developed an aversion to riding Quarter Horses. Even before the accident, I had appreciated the endurance and spirit of the Arabian breed, and had used Arabians a great deal on the Crown Ranch. But after Little John wrecked my back, I came to appreciate another quality in Arabian horses: they were kinder to my back than Quarter Horses.

Perhaps I should qualify this by saying that I have ridden Arabians that were rough-gaited and some Quarter Horses that were smooth. There are exceptions on both sides, but as a general rule, I have found Arabians to be less jarring. I assume this has something to do with the differences in the anatomy and musculature of the two breeds. Quarter Horses are more massive than Arabians, particularly in the shoulders and hindquarters, and this allows them to make the kind of sudden moves that win money in cutting-horse competitions. Arabians are not nearly as adept at cutting. In most cowboy circles, this is considered a liability, but I came to appreciate it.

While I was working for the Ellzeys, who kept a string of twelve or thirteen Quarter Horses, I seldom rode LZ horses, using instead my half-Arabian mare Calipso day after day. I still suffered from some chronic back trouble, especially when we were roping cattle in the pasture, but I was able to function with occasional visits to the chiropractor.

This book comes from the journals I kept during my two years as an LZ cowboy, and I should explain why I chose to present the material in the journal format. I have always kept journals of my ranch work. By the time I took the Crown Ranch job in 1974, I had begun to suspect that my cowboy experiences would play an important role in my future work as an author, although I didn't anticipate just how important it would become. That didn't make itself known to me until about 1977 or 1978, when I stumbled into the realization that I was most comfortable telling stories in the voice of a cowboy—and later, of course, in the voice of a certain ranch dog.

At that point I began devoting more time to the journal entries, recording the small details and mundane events of my life as a cowboy. As a result, my journal entries on the Barby Ranch were more detailed than those I made on the Crown Ranch, and those I wrote on the LZ Ranch were more complete than the Beaver River entries.

If someone had asked what I intended to do with my LZ journals, I would have said that they would serve me as reference material. At some later date when I wanted to do a book on my experiences, I would go through the journals and pull out individual incidents and rewrite them as stories, using the entries as field notes to supply me with facts and details. That is what I did in writing *Panhandle Cowboy*, *The Modern Cowboy*, and *Cowboy Country*. I wrote all those books while the characters, horses, and events were still fresh in my memory, but I also made good use of my journals.

I always thought that I would eventually write the same kind of book about the LZ Ranch experiences, but Hank the Cowdog changed my plans. In the fall of 1982 I started my own publishing company, Maverick Books, in Perryton. In the spring of 1983 we brought out the first Hank the Cowdog book—which, I confess, seemed nothing special or out of the ordinary to me. But the public liked that dog and demanded more, and by the middle of 1984 my future as an author had been determined for me. Increasingly, the reading public was thinking of me as the author of the Hank books, and no one seemed particularly interested that I wrote nonfiction books about cowboying. That was fine with me because by that time, I had figured out that an author could starve to death writing good books about his cowboy experiences. I had a wife and three children to support, and I also had a strong aversion to starving.

I followed the advice of my audience and have never regretted it, but one result of this change in direction was that I put away the LZ journals and didn't look at them again until the winter of 1993. During a long spell of snowy weather, I was looking for something to read and thought it might be fun to see what Tom Ellzey and I had been doing during the winter of 1979. The gap of a dozen years was enough to place me in the position of an objective reader, someone who didn't know what was coming next. I read the material with great interest, and at some point it occurred to me that these stories didn't need to be rewritten—and shouldn't be. They should be presented exactly as I wrote them, as "the log of a cowboy," to borrow a term from Andy Adams.

This surprised me because I had never even considered using the journal format for an entire book because . . . well, a journal was too haphazard, chaotic, harum-scarum to be of interest to a reader. Readers responded to form and structure and movement. My theories of storytelling rebelled at the notion of using field notes as a finished product. It didn't seem right, just as it wouldn't be right for a carpenter to leave rough two-by-four studs showing in a new house. Yet I enjoyed reading the LZ journals *just as they were*, even though they lacked the structure and polish of a finished story. What gave the entries their strength was the integrity of the experiences. If a reader wanted to find out how it felt to be a cowboy in the Texas Panhandle in the years 1979–81, here it was: the snow, the mud, the cattle drives, the pranks, the accidents, the equipment, the horses, the frustrations, the triumphs.

But most of all, it was the story of two men, Tom Ellzey and me, who took pride in our horsemanship, our roping, and the hard work we did day after day. And it suddenly occurred to me, "This is interesting stuff. Does anyone do these things anymore? Do people still work this hard? Does anyone still care about the things that mattered so much to us?" That's when I decided that the LZ material should stay just as I wrote it, with just a little bit of editing.

One last word about the LZ Ranch. Since so much of my identity and reputation are bound up with Hank the Cowdog, it might interest the reader to know that there is a very close connection between the LZ Ranch and the Hank stories. I was cowboying for the Ellzeys when I wrote the first Hank story in 1981. The ranch I have in mind when I write the Hank stories is the Ellzey ranch, and Hank scholars who read this book will recognize certain names and locations: Tuerto, Drover, and Casey the Bronc; the machine shed, the calf shed, the sick pen, the gas tanks, and so forth.

Three of the human characters in the Hank stories—High Loper, Sally May, and Slim—were originally patterned after Tom Ellzey, Janet Ellzey, and myself, and many of the incidents you will read about in this book have found their way into Hank the Cowdog adventures. As you can see, those two years I spent as an LZ cowboy were important to me, and I am grateful to the Ellzeys for the many ways they contributed to my development. I am also grateful to Kris, my wife of twenty-nine years, who has shared all my hardships and adventures. Had she not followed me and Tom through mud, snow, and summer heat, we would not have a photographic record of these experiences.

M Cross Ranch
Roberts County, Texas

Corrals at LZ Headquarters, with Wolf Creek in the background.

September 5, 1979

I have been on the LZ almost a month now. I haven't made any entries in this journal for two reasons. First, I don't have the time to do it. My days begin between 4:30 and 5:30, when I go down to my office in Perryton and do my daily writing on the books I'm working on. I leave for the ranch at 8:00 and don't get back home until 7:00 or 8:00 at night. There isn't much slack time in there for journal entries. Second, the work is hard and steady, but none of it, up to now, has been particularly noteworthy. I have spent a lot of time on a horse this past month, prowling pastures, moving cattle around, and such, but the work has been fairly routine.

Yesterday I rode four pastures. In the Lower Section West I found a lot of pinkeye. Up on the Beaver River, I would have been carrying medicine and I would've roped and doctored on the spot. I haven't felt free to do that yet on the LZ. I don't want the boss to think I'm a hot-dog roper who's here to play rodeo with his cattle.

But yesterday I found a steer calf that was stone blind. He was up on the north end of the pasture by himself, and he couldn't see anything. Both eyes were inflamed and ulcerated. I tried to drive him back to the herd, but when I saw that he was blind, I decided to take him to the corral and doctor him up right. So I took down my rope.

I was riding an LZ horse named Deuce. He's a sorrel with good size and cutting ability, but he is headstrong and wants to run. I had a hard time holding him back and the calf made a poor target. He dodged and stumbled, as blind cattle will

1

do. I made a throw and it was right on target, but I didn't get my slack jerked up in time and he ran through my loop.

As I was building another loop, he ran straight toward a sheer cliff above Cottonwood Creek and went over. I thought for a second that Deuce, who follows cattle well, was going to go with him, but I got him shut down on the edge of the cliff. It must have been twenty feet straight down. What a surprise that must have been! The calf flew through the air and crashed into the water. I thought for sure he had broken his leg or neck, but after staggering around for a while, he seemed to recover.

I rode around and found a path down to the creek bottom, and started the calf east, toward the Lower Section pens. When we got up on flat ground, I roped him and drove him across Wolf Creek. I tied him to a tree by Skip Ellzey's house and went for the stock trailer.

One day last week, I roped three steers and loaded them into the trailer. I had a hard time catching them. I caught one on the first loop but wasted three loops on the others. These were all sick animals, and they tended to dodge and run in circles, and they didn't run very fast. I think sick cattle are harder to rope than healthy ones.

September 6, 1979

The story of the blind calf had a happy ending. We kept him up for the night so that we could doctor him twice before we turned him out. Yesterday morning, Tom gave him an injection on both eyeballs and we glued patches over both eyes to protect them from sunlight. We figured he wouldn't be any blinder with the patches than he was without them. Then I loaded him in the trailer and took him back to the pasture.

Since I'd found him alone the day before, I was afraid that he might have lost his mother and that she had gone dry. My major objective was to find the cow. Without a mother, the calf could starve down and maybe die. I pulled into the pasture and bawled like a calf, then I got out to lock in the front hubs so that I could ford the creek in four-wheel drive. Before I got back into the pickup, I heard a cow bawling, and a big horned cow came out of the trees. When the calf heard the cow, he blatted. I turned him out and he went straight to her and began nursing. That was a nice ending.

Yesterday, Lawrence and I gathered thirty-five cows and thirty calves off a cane field and drove them to the Lower Section pens. That was pretty good work for two riders, but we got it done and didn't spill a critter. We cut off the weaning calves and hauled them to the upper place, and then we doctored several for pinkeye and ticks. We worked them through an old wooden chute, and one of them, a black bald-faced heifer with pinkeye, broke out into the arena. When we finished with the others, we rode out into the arena and tried to pen the heifer with her mother. She was waspy and didn't want to go into the corral.

Lawrence said we might have to rope her, though he preferred that we didn't. We held the cow and calf in front of the gate and built loops in our ropes. The heifer ran back and forth, while Lawrence stewed and yelled. We were tired and wanted to be done. He said, "Let's try to get her through the gate but if she breaks back, put a rope on her."

He turned the heifer and she came my way, with her bad eye toward me. Since she was blind in that eye, I didn't want to get too close to her, for fear she would trip Calipso. She went to the fence and started west at a run. I couldn't turn her, so I fell in behind her and started swinging my rope. I dropped the loop over her head but she ran through it. When I got my slack, I had two heels. I held on and took my dally.

I really didn't think I would end up with anything. Usually the calf kicks out of it. But I got her and put her on the ground. Lawrence went for the medicine. When he got back, I threw a double half-hitch over the saddle horn and climbed off to hold the calf while he doctored her eyes. Lawrence asked if Calipso could hold the rope tight, knowing that if she let any slack in the rope, the calf would kick out and we would have it all to do again. To tell the truth, I didn't know if she would hold it or not. I had worked calves on the ground before but I didn't know whether I had done it enough so that she was trained to keep a tight rope. But I said I thought she would, and by George, she did. She kept the rope tight and performed like a little pro. I was proud of her. And I think the boss was impressed.

I felt mighty good after this. It was the first time the boss had ever seen me rope under range conditions, and it went well. Now he knows that I can handle myself, that I can get the job done right, and that I've got a good horse working for me.

This has been an odd year. We had a wet spring, a wet summer, and have had very little hot weather. August has been pretty dry, but that is not unusual. Wolf Creek is deep and has lots of water in the holes, though it has some dry spots in the Lower Section. Sunflowers, ironweed, and other weeds are tall, and that probably contributes to the pinkeye problem. It is getting bad along the creek, and I wish we could doctor pinkeye twice a week. The grass is wonderful, and I have heard Lawrence say that he has never seen a better grass year. In fifty years he has seen the sunflowers worse only once.

Tom's last cutting of alfalfa is on the ground, and yesterday the people from New Holland brought out a hay stacker. If it works, I expect he will buy it: $6,500. He has concluded that hauling hay on a truck is too slow, too hard on the help. He is right about that, and I'll be glad to be spared the torment of hauling hay in the broiling sun. Yet, in a way, I hate to see the old ways pass. Hay-hauling was grueling work, but it was also a challenge. It tested a man, took him to the limits of his endurance. I always hate to surrender human functions to a machine.

But I have a bad back. Tom has a bad back and a bum wrist. We have a lot of work to do and we don't have the time to handle every bale by hand. I guess it will be a change for the better.

September 9, 1979

Yesterday Lawrence and I were cutting cattle in the arena at the Lower Section. One old horned cow refused to leave. We took her back and forth and she kept breaking back on us. Since she had long sharp horns, and seemed inclined to use them, we didn't want to work her in close quarters.

Finally Lawrence had had enough. He pulled down his rope, slipped the knot over his horn, and dropped the loop over her head. He pulled on her with Happy, and I got behind her and whipped her with my rope.

We got her outside and I told the boss to drag her to an open space, away from the pickups, and I would heel her and stretch her out. That's the way we did it up on the Beaver River. We team-roped the cattle, so that the heeler could hold the animal down while the header took off his rope. But Lawrence comes from a different tradition of roping, where the cowboy ties his rope solid to the horn and doesn't depend on a heeler. Team-roping is not a technique he has used in his career, and he doesn't have much faith in it. He said no to the heeling idea. He thought the cow was tired enough so that he could walk up to her and take off the rope.

I didn't say anything. I knew that I could heel her and that this was by far the best, easiest and safest way to get the rope off her head, but there was no use in trying to argue with him. I didn't want to get close to those big horns, but if Lawrence wanted to, that was fine with me. I got off Calipso and sat on Happy while the boss walked down the rope. He didn't get within ten feet of the wild hussy before she snorted and ran, making menacing gestures with her horns. She did this twice and it became clear that she wasn't going to stand there and let him take off the rope. With a sigh, the boss said he guessed we would have to heel her down.

I got on Calipso and laid a nice open loop in front of her back legs. Lawrence pulled the cow a few steps. She walked into the loop with both feet. I pulled slack, dallied, and pulled her down with Calipso. Skip Ellzey was there and took off the head rope. In twenty seconds we were done. This incident made me aware of the advantage a dally roper has over a hard-and-fast roper. A roper who is tied solid to the horn would have to deal with thirty feet of slack, whereas I just dallied short and turned away from the cow.

September 12, 1979

Several days ago I went over to the Lower Section East to check the cattle. I had seen pinkeye in the calves a week before and I knew they needed attention. Right away I found a steer calf that had a patch over his right eye, and he had gone blind in his left.

I went after him but couldn't get a shot. He ran in typical blind-calf fashion, dodging at every little sound, weaving, darting, stumbling. I didn't want to get too close to him and elected to wait for a good shot. He ran in circles for awhile, then broke to the east, heading straight for the fence between Ellzeys and the Johnny Daniels Ranch. I knew that if he ever hit the fence, he would run through it, and I would have a nice mess on my hands: a blind calf separated from his mother and running loose in the neighbor's pasture.

I spurred Calipso, got ahead of the calf, and tried to turn him west by yelling and making noise. It didn't work. He hit the fence and went through. The wires tripped him for just a moment, then he was on the other side, and scared enough to run for another hour.

I had a loop built in my rope. I knew I would have one shot. If I missed, I would spend the next hour looking for him in the weeds, tall grass, and trees along Wolf Creek. I remained calm and didn't hurry my throw, because hurrying messes up my roping worse than anything. I tossed out a soft loop and nailed him. I threw a half hitch over the horn, and while Calipso held the calf on the west side, I went through the fence, flanked him, tied him down with a pigging string, and doctored his eyes. The eye that had been patched was healed up, so I just moved the patch over to the other eye. I carried medicine, glue, and patches in my saddle bags.

I doctored three more small calves in that pasture and caught them all on the first loop. I was proud. I think my roping, both heading and heeling, has improved since I started working here. I don't know why. I guess I've had quite a bit of practice, come to think of it.

I am beginning to get a feel for the roping techniques I learned from the cowboys on the Beaver River. It has taken awhile to soak in.

September 14, 1979

Last Wednesday I rode pastures all day, including three north of the creek where we have taken the steers that are straightened out. The Ellzey strategy is to keep the new cattle close to home until they are dehorned, castrated, healed up and healthy, and then we take them up into the north pastures.

While I was riding the north pastures, I found four cases
of pinkeye that needed attention. I was carrying medicine
when I found them and possibly could have doctored them,
but I hesitated to attempt it myself. These steers were big,
between 450 and 650 pounds, and it would be much easier
to approach them with another man and team-rope them.

I told Tom about it, and Thursday afternoon he saddled
up Happy and I saddled Calipso, and we trailered our horses
over to the West Pasture. Tom felt apprehensive about using
the team-roping approach. It's not something the Ellzeys
have used in the pasture. Heading and heeling is a dally
technique, and the Ellzey ranch has been a hard-and-fast
outfit for more than sixty years. Tom was uneasy about it
but he was willing to give it a try.

It was a beautiful fall afternoon, not too hot and not too
cool, just right for long-sleeve shirts and felt hats. We found
the cattle in one of the canyons in the West Pasture and
pushed them down to the windmill where the ground was
flat and not so much covered with rock. We looked them over
and picked out the steers with the worst pinkeye.

Tom was tied solid. I, of course, would dally. Tom took
the first throw and missed. I moved in, cut the steer out of
the bunch, and got after him. I made a bad throw and missed.
I was nervous and hurried my shot. Tom got after the steer
again and made a good throw, only the steer ran through the
loop. I was right behind him, moved in, and put the loop
around the steer's neck. Tom heeled him down. We put my
head rope on the steer's front hocks and stretched him out.

John Erickson and Tom Ellzey preparing to rope and doctor cattle on the ranch. The first man roped the head, the second took the heels.

He had very bad pinkeye. He was blind on the right side and his eye was ulcerated and white. Tom had brought along all the equipment he needed for a complete treatment: medicine, syringe, blue spray, and eye patches and glue.

I had never heard of anyone giving the delicate injection under the skin of the eyeball out in the pasture, and I wasn't sure it could be done. I doubt that I would have attempted it, but Tom did, and he had a much easier time of it than he would have working with a squeeze chute. We discovered that when the critter is stretched out between two horses, with all four feet contained, he can't throw his head. I don't know why, but it seems to be true.

We gave the fellow the full treatment and went looking for the next one. We found him near the windmill. He moved from left to right in front of Tom, and Tom nailed him with a perfect shot. He pulled him out of the tall grass and weeds and I heeled him. Tom got down and gave him the full treatment. By this time he could see that team-roping cattle in the pasture was an easy and practical way of handling them. And it was also *fun*.

We spotted another steer with runny eyes, and I got after him. He was running beside another steer and it wasn't an easy shot, but I stuck it on him on the first throw. Tom whooped and yelled. He thought it was a nice piece of roping, and congratulated me. He heeled the steer, we stretched him out and doctored his eyes.

By this time, Tom's spirits were soaring. This was his first introduction to team-roping and he was delighted with the results. We were getting the cattle roped quickly, were not running them all over the pasture, and were putting them on the ground without much fuss or strain.

We loaded our horses and trailered over to the Northwest Pasture and found another steer with bad pinkeye. Tom missed his first throw. It was not a good shot, too long, and I think Happy was cheating him and wasn't moving in close enough. I was right behind him and opened up little Calipso. We chased the steer for fifty yards or so, and I didn't throw until I had a good shot. I nailed him and dallied up. Tom came in with his heel loop and we bedded him down.

We saw another steer with watery eyes and went after him. I made a pretty good throw but pulled my slack too soon and only caught his nose. Tom and Hap got after him and Tom stuck it on. We went home at sundown, feeling like a pair of pretty good cowboys.

On Saturday, two days later, we gathered the Home Pasture and sorted off fifty-one yearling bulls that needed to be castrated. Some of them were huge, in the 600–700 pound range. We were dreading the thought of using one heeler and tailing them down by hand. Tom had already made up his mind that we were going to head and heel them. After our pasture work on Thursday, he knew we could do it and that this was the easiest way to handle big stock. But he wasn't sure Lawrence would approve.

That morning, Tom casually mentioned that we had team-roped some steers in the pasture on Thursday. Lawrence didn't ask how it had gone but blurted, "Well, that's fun but it's sure hard on cattle." My blood pressure began to rise. Tom said nothing. Just before lunch, Tom and I sorted off eleven of the biggest bulls and put them in the back lot. He still intended to team-rope them, whether the boss approved of it or not. After lunch, we went to work, team-roping the bulls.

Roping those big bulls was a good deal harder than what we had done in the pasture. The bulls were much stronger than the steers had been. They were as strong as grown cows, and it was harder to rope in a confined area than in the pasture. Also, we were under some pressure, since we had gotten the impression that the boss thought we were a couple of rookie cowboys who wanted to play with their ropes.

Tom headed and I heeled the first two bulls. Then I headed the next one. This ox was so big and stout that Calipso, an Arabian mare who weighed maybe 800 or 900 pounds, couldn't handle him. She braced all four of her skinny legs and tried to hold her ground, but she couldn't pull the ox far enough to give Tom his heel shot. We decided then and there that we had better let Happy take care of the heading, and let me and Calipso do the heeling. Even so, it wasn't easy work. Tom had to get down and throw several of the bulls because Calipso just didn't have enough brawn to pull them down. I love to ride Arabian horses, but there is no denying that in this kind of work, they are inferior to the bigger Quarter Horses.

John and Calipso on the head, Tom and Happy on the heels. Here, Tom has dismounted and is preparing to put John's rope on the steer's front feet.

By the time we had worked these big brutes Lawrence had decided that team-roping was the best method. He wasn't prepared to give his blanket approval of the technique in general, but we had convinced him that we could handle the big stuff better with two horses than with one.

But the next time we do this, I might use one of the LZ Quarter Horses, maybe Popeye who weighs about 1300.

After working these eleven big bulls, we worked twenty smaller ones in the traditional manner, with Lawrence heeling and Tom and me tailing them down. We had one baldface bull that tried to fight. Lawrence caught him by both hocks, and immediately the bull charged his horse. He had horns and was big enough to hurt someone. He made a couple of passes at Tom and me, and I suggested that we catch his head. I got a rope and stuck it on him. We dallied to a corral post and stretched him out, and that was all the trouble he caused.

Lawerence had to leave at 6:00 P.M. to attend a meeting in town. No sooner had he pulled away than Tom and I went back to heading and heeling. It went smoothly. These cattle were smaller than the first bunch, and we roped and cut until it was too dark to see. And we had us one heck of a good time.

October 1, 1979

Last week Tom and I took a whole day to do nothing but ride pastures and look at the cattle. We rode eleven pastures, counted everything, and doctored what needed it. We carried our medicine bag with us, with everything we needed to treat even the most severe cases of pinkeye. In the West Pasture we doctored only one out of 110 steers. Tom slipped up on him at the windmill and noosed him before he got the news. I used my stiff nylon and double-hocked him. In the Middle Pasture we rode through the cattle at the windmill. We worked them quietly and roped and doctored three calves without ever getting them into a run.

We figured out that Tom is better at roping in a herd than I am. He is good at making long shots, and since he is tied solid, he doesn't mind throwing to the end of his rope. I am better at the running shots. I am most accurate when I get an animal that is running hard and straight.

From the Middle Pasture we went to the Lower Section East and doctored two calves, then to the Lower Section West. We each roped one calf and never got them out of a walk. We nailed them both on the first loop. Tom roped his calf deep, however, and the rope got behind his shoulders. He was a big stout 500-pound steer and he was actually jerking Happy around. I had a heck of a time putting my rope on his head. When I got close enough for a shot, I was close enough to get caught in Tom's rope. It was a difficult case, but we took care of it.

Next, we had to doctor a cow who was blind in one eye. Tom took the heading job, since he was mounted on the stouter horse. Right off, the cow ran through a fence into the Dutcher Creek Pasture. Tom was nervous and tight. He was a little worried about roping a grown cow, I suppose. He missed his first loop because Happy didn't put him up close enough. On the second, he just made a bad throw. But he caught her on the third toss. We laid her down and we did our job.

I am amazed that, all at once, I have become fairly accurate with a rope. About three weeks ago everything seemed to jell and I was doing everything right. I pointed my finger and dipped my loop on the head shots, and all at once I couldn't miss. It's a great feeling, because I have known many days of humiliation in the roping business.

Today I bought a grass rope at Stockman's Supply. I want to try it and see how it works. I've never used a grass rope before. It is a soft rope with a good feel to it, and if I can learn to use it, it will cut down on my problem of jerking slack on small calves. This loop ought to smear all over a small calf.

October 6, 1979

There is no end to the work on the LZ. We have enough work to keep four men busy. We haven't planted the wheat yet. We need to fix some pasture fence. We need to put electric fence around several patches of volunteer wheat. We have steers in the Home Pasture that should be dehorned, and others that are dehorned and should be checked for maggots. Then there are the routine jobs: riding pastures and doctoring pinkeye; checking windmills; riding the Home Pasture every other day; working with Tom's filly; feeding, doctoring, on and on. On top of all this, we need to check out the running gear on all three stock trailers. And Tom is try-

Lawrence Ellzey, the boss, at quittin' time.

ing to build a room onto his house, and we are getting in a lot of new cattle.

Last Wednesday Lawrence went to the Beaver Livestock Auction and brought back sixty-two steers and bulls. Yesterday we received forty-eight four-weight cattle. We have to keep them in the corrals for a week until they get weaned and straightened out. Then we turn them out into the Home Pasture and we'll have to watch them closely. Many of these calves must be dehorned and castrated before they can be moved to wheat, and all of that takes time and work.

As I say, there's no end to it. We have our list of things to do but we usually end up responding to emergencies as they happen. The day is never long enough, the week is always too short. I think this used to bother Tom, but he has learned to find his natural pace and do all he can.

We had a cool summer and an especially cool August, but September and October have been unusually warm. We had several ninety-degree days in September, and at least one day over a hundred.

October 12, 1979

We spent most of the last two days branding and doctoring the new cattle. We had more than a hundred at one time and every pen was filled. At this stage we have to watch them closely for signs of sickness. I pulled one out of the pen last Saturday afternoon, gave him a shot, and put him into the sick pen. By Sunday noon he was dead. There went about four hundred dollars.

Yesterday I got all the cattle branded and out on grass, leaving a few suspicious characters up for more medication. The heck of it is that they *all* look sick. If we had doctored the usual symptoms—coughing and snotty nose—we would have doctored almost all of them. The corrals are very dusty and all the cattle look bad. To add to our woes, the days are hot and the nights are chilly. That's pneumonia weather. I've been riding the Home Pasture every day, looking for sick ones, and I've brought one home every time I've been out.

October 18, 1979

Tom received another load of cattle over the weekend. Ned Kygar, the fellow who runs the Beaver Livestock Auction, called and said he had bought a set of yearlings in the eighty to eighty-five cent/pound range. He thought they were worth the money, so Tom told him to bring them down.

So it was back to branding and doctoring. Out of the hundred head that we have turned out in the past week, four have died. Tom found them all in the pasture between Friday and Sunday. None had been kept up for medicine, which means that they didn't show any symptoms until five to seven days after they went out on grass. One of their problems might be the dust in the corrals. It is terrible right now.

We rounded up the Home Pasture yesterday, cut off six or seven sick ones, and sorted off thirty-four head to take up to the north pastures. These are cattle that have been castrated, dehorned, and straightened out. This leaves us with about seventy-five in the Home Pasture to dehorn and castrate. We still have about twenty Kygar cattle in the lots to brand and turn out, and we will have to ride the Home Pasture every day to look for sick ones.

After we gathered the Home Pasture, we were seven short on our count. We went back and found three before lunch, then after lunch I rode the creek again and found one red yearling. He was thin and lethargic, didn't look well. He must have been lying down somewhere when we rounded up. I started driving him toward the house. As we went I practiced with my new grass rope. I had never carried it on the saddle before, and if this beast gave me any trouble, I was going to use it on him.

He didn't want to go to the corrals, and he took evasive action. He went down to the creek, just west of the Parnell Crossing. I drove him out and pointed him west. Instead of going up the bank and getting back on flat ground, he followed the creek.

The bank became steeper, and to my left the creek changed from shallows to a hole that was fairly wide and deep. The steer continued on this course until he ran out of path. He was trapped between a steep bank to his right and a four- to five-foot dropoff above the creek. When he could no longer take a step forward, he fell off into the creek. The water was deep enough so that his head went under and he had to swim out.

I started to turn Calipso around. She lost her footing. The bank caved off and she—we, actually—fell into the creek backwards. I didn't see it coming and didn't expect it, but my reactions were good. I kicked out of the stirrups and got as far away from her as I could. I went into the water up to my neck, though when I got my feet on the bottom it was only waist deep. Calipso floundered around in the water, striking it with her front hooves, until she discovered she could stand. She stood quietly until I led her out. I was wearing my heavy Grampy Buck spurs and both my boots were filled with water. I was soaked from my chin down.

My grass rope got wet and became as hard as a nylon heeling rope. My saddle was wet from top to bottom. I didn't have time to pull off my boots and pour out the water, since the steer was moving up the creek and I didn't want to lose him in the brush. I mounted up and took him on to the corrals.

Fortunately, the day was fairly warm, about seventy degrees, so I didn't get chilled. But as soon as I had penned the steer, I went streaking up to Tom's house. I had so much suction in my boots that getting them off was a problem. I'm not sure I could have done it without a boot jack. Tom donated some dry clothes to the cause, and fifteen minutes later, we were back at work.

October 25, 1979

Two days ago Clarence Herrington, the cowboy on the Lazy Y Ranch, got hit in the head with the gate lever of a squeeze chute. I guess it really knocked a slat out of him. Bill Herndon took him to the hospital and got him stitched up. I met him on the road yesterday, as I was driving out to the LZ Ranch, and stopped to talk. He wore a big gauze bandage around his head—no hat or glasses. His hair was sticking out around the bandage and his left eye had a purple area under it. He looked like a Civil War veteran.

Yesterday we rounded up the two north pastures. Tom started gathering the bunch in the Northeast while Janet and I rounded up the Northwest. Tom found a *sheep* in the pasture, and naturally he felt compelled to rope it. He said it didn't run very fast and it wasn't a hard shot. At noon we tied it with a pigging string and hauled it back to Headquarters on the back of the flatbed pickup.

We have no idea where a sheep came from in this sheepless country, or how it has survived in an area that is loaded with hungry coyotes.

We are running the Home Pasture steers on alfalfa now, and every evening Tom and I have to drive them off the alfalfa and back onto grass. Otherwise, they would bloat on the alfalfa. To entertain ourselves while we're moving the steers, we practice roping their rear ends.

October 31, 1979

Two days ago we had shirt-sleeve weather, mid or high seventies. That night a norther moved in and yesterday morning it was drizzling rain, cloudy, chilly, and windy. By noon the wind was blowing harder and the temperature was dropping like a rock. Around 1:00 I went out on a horse to check the Home Pasture steers and look for sick ones. I wore plenty of clothes and a slicker.

It started raining hard, a cold wind-driven rain. My glasses got covered and I could hardly see. The cattle were all humped up and miserable, and I couldn't tell a sick one from the ones that were well. I was riding Happy and he didn't want to go north into that stinging rain. I wasn't out more than thirty minutes but I got soaked. The weather got worse by the hour. By 4:00 the rain turned to sleet, and by 5:30 it was snowing. Around 9:00 that night the electricity went out in Perryton. I heard that it was out in the whole northern Panhandle. It didn't go back on until 3:00 the next afternoon.

This morning I got up in a cold house, put on my red long-john underwear, and all my warmest clothes, and went to work without any coffee. Tom and I lit a fire in his wood stove and were drinking a cup of hot coffee when Lawrence called from town and said that we had some steers out up on the flats.

While Tom hooked up the big gooseneck trailer, I gathered the horses and saddled four of them: one each for me, Tom, Lawrence, and Nathan, Tom's teenage son. Then we drove up to the flats on the Osborne place. We had an electric fence around this wheat field, and the charger ran on 110-volt current. When the power went out, so did the electric fence, and our steers had drifted a mile or two southeast. We found them in some volunteer wheat.

The clouds had mostly cleared away, but the wind was frigid. The temperature must have been around thirty-five degrees, with a chill factor close to zero. We rode out into the field which had taken two to three inches of slow rain in the last twenty-four hours. Calipso staggered through the mud. I never got her out of a walk, and I'm not sure I could have. She could barely walk.

That done, we ate a quick lunch in town and headed for the ranch. Tom and I rode the Home Pasture and found three sick steers. We roped them and put them in the trailer. We caught all three on the first loop, and none ever got out of a walk.

November 5, 1979

Last Wednesday afternoon Tom and I saddled up and
trailered our horses to the Four Corners corral. Lawrence
had found a buyer for the big end of the steers, 124 head
that weighed around 750 pounds. These were steers that
had summered in the north pastures and he wanted us to
bring them down to the Home Pasture so that on shipping
day, we could ease them into the corral with very little shrink.
We gathered them up and started driving them down
toward Headquarters, three miles to the south. They were
gentle and we got them trail-broke in no time. We took them
through the Southeast Pasture.

John and Calipso riding pastures.

Along the way and while they were strung out in a long line, we had to cut out four small steers that belonged in the Southeast. These four wanted to stay with the bigger steers and they followed us all the way to the gate into the Middle Pasture. We threw the big steers into the Middle and pointed them south, down the fence. Then we had to go back and chase those four little steers a half-mile to the windmill.

We had to ride hard to catch up with the main herd. We put them into the Home Pasture and drove them to water, then fed them thirty-two bales of alfalfa hay. It was 4:00 by then and we still had a lot of work to do. With the shipping steers now in the Home Pasture, we didn't have any place to go with the lighter steers on alfalfa. They had to be driven off the alfalfa every night because rain or heavy dew on green alfalfa will cause cattle to bloat and die. Hence, we had to build an electric fence around a little patch of grass on the south end of the alfalfa field, then run the steers onto the grass for the night.

We ran out of daylight. At dark we were still building the fence, and by the time we got it built and charged, it was so dark that we couldn't see anything. And we still had to run the cattle off the alfalfa and put them into the grass trap. We feared that they might run though the electric fence in the dark, but we had to do something with them.

Tom and I drove back to Headquarters, saddled up again, and rode our horses back to the alfalfa field. There was no moon and we couldn't see where we were going. Lawrence was in the field with his pickup, and he shone his headlights on the gate. Otherwise, we might not have found it.

Next, we had to find the steers and push them to the south end, onto the grass. We could hear the cattle moving in the alfalfa but we couldn't see them, even when they were standing beside us. Tom's dog Sadie was in the field, and several times I fell in behind her, thinking she was a steer.

At last we cleared the field and got all the steers, 155 head, down to the south end. Lawrence positioned himself so that his lights were on the gate, and we pushed them into the trap. They started moving in, slowly at first. Then they boogered at something and stampeded.

Tom and I went into a high lope and tried to slow them. They were on one side of the electric fence and we were on the other. We soon rode out of the light and found ourselves plunging through inky darkness. It was spooky. We could hear the stampede but could see nothing—not the cattle, the fence, the ground, or each other. We couldn't get the cattle stopped and they plowed over the electric fence. We heard the wire twang and Tom started cursing in his loudest voice. We had spent several hours building that fence and they had wrecked it in less than two minutes.

We were all cold and tired and hungry and in a foul mood, but we had to get the cattle off the alfalfa. We decided to throw them into a field of volunteer wheat to the east and hold them there for the night, until we could make a better arrangement. We rounded them up again in the dark, only now we had to worry about that electric-fence wire. We didn't know whether it was still on the posts or if it had been broken and dragged out into the alfalfa. We sure didn't want to ride our horses into the wire and get ourselves bucked off, and maybe garroted in the wire. Our horses were a little humpy in the cold anyway. We managed to get the job done and make it home at 8:30.

The next morning was cold, gray, and rainy. We had to doctor the sick pen, then go over and rebuild the electric fence. It rained hard on us and by noon my black felt hat was completely soaked up and weighed about three pounds. Water was dripping down my neck from inside the hat. I was rather demoralized and didn't enjoy slogging through the rain and mud. This was not the romantic side of cowboying, and I found myself wondering why I had ever gone into this business.

At lunch we had a good time, though. Lawrence wanted to call a man in town about some wheat pasture. He didn't have his reading glasses and asked me to look up the number in the phone book. Big mistake. I gave him the number of the Sheriff's Department.

When Lawrence said, "Who? Sheriff's Department! Well, excuse me," Tom and I laughed until we hurt. The boss growled about smart aleck cowboys.

November 8, 1979

Yesterday, Saturday, we delivered and shipped the 124 steers. When Lawrence and I went to the Dutch Inn for breakfast, it was snowing. With this wet snow on top of the rain of two days ago, we wondered if the cattle trucks could get to the corrals to load.

They did, arriving at 9:00 as scheduled. Tom and I gathered the steers and never got them out of a walk. They were full and had very little shrink. When we started loading the trucks, Jerry Stubblefield, the buyer, came into the corral with us. He was buying the steers for a man in Iowa. It was snowing hard by this time and the mud in the corrals was six inches deep.

We joked back and forth with Jerry. He complained that the cattle were too full and that he was going to pay $.765/ pound for half a ton of ice and snow on the backs of the steers.

Lawrence pointed to a Hereford steer with an orange tag in his ear. We had removed these old ear tags on the others but somehow we had missed this one. Sometimes we used ear tags to mark animals that were prone to bloat, but that wasn't the case on this one. Lawrence assured Jerry that there was nothing wrong with the steer. The boss was so solemn about this, I couldn't resist teasing him.

"You mean that bloater? Oh, he'll be all right, Jerry. Shucks, we've let him down so many times with a rubber hose, the minute you walk into the corral, he'll open his mouth and say 'aaah.'"

Everyone but Lawrence thought this was funny. He was afraid that Jerry would believe us, which of course would have cast doubt on the boss's integrity. The boss turned to me and rumbled, "If one of those steers turns out to be a bloater, they're going to think we threw him into the bunch, and *you boys are going to hear about it.*"

When Lawrence mentioned to Stubblefield that he would have another hundred steers ready to sell in a few weeks, I said, "Oh yeah, that's the *real* junk on the ranch—pinkeyes, bloaters, cripples. Five of those steers are getting around on crutches and several of 'em are so blind that they're having to use seeing-eye dogs."

We all roared with laughter. Lawrence shook his head. He knew he didn't have a chance.

November 17, 1979

Several days ago Tom and I saddled up the horses and trailered over to the Middle Pasture. We knew that several critters had strayed out of the Home Pasture and into the Middle, and we wanted to gather them up.

We found the herd on the north end, up near the Four Corners corral. One of the strays was a black bull that weighed 500–550 pounds. Several weeks before, we had driven him out of the Middle Pasture, and moments later, he hopped back over the fence. He had caused us a lot of trouble and we were out to get him.

We unloaded the horses and worked the strays out of the herd. There were two of them, the black bull and a thin Hereford steer. We headed them toward the corral. They didn't want to go and tried their best to cut back on us. We had our ropes down and were just itching for a good excuse to use them. But alas, they went into the corral and we shut the gate behind them.

We rode back to the pickup and trailer, loaded our horses, and drove to the corral to load up the steers. As we backed the trailer up to the loading chute, the black bull walked up to the wire gate and hopped over it. The other steer followed.

They weren't mad or excited. They just knew that the gate couldn't hold them, and away they went.

We weren't entirely unhappy about this. We hit the saddles and went after them. It soon became clear that they weren't going back to the corral. The bull cut between us and Tom made a long throw with his rope. It hit the bull on the head, closed around his nose, and pulled off.

"Rope him!" Tom yelled. Calipso and I chased him up a draw. She gave me a perfect shot and I fired. I caught his neck and one front leg. I thought he was going to be a fighter, so I decided to take some of the fight out of him. When I jerked my slack, he stopped. I rode past him, dallied, and hit the rope with a full head of steam. His feet went straight up in the air and hit the ground. When he got up, I spurred Calipso into a lope and we threw him again. When I let him up, he headed straight for the corral. He wanted no more of that.

Thanksgiving Day, 1979

Yesterday was cold and windy, with the high temperature around thirty-five degrees and the wind hitting thirty-five miles per hour. Tom, his cousin David Ellzey, and I built electric fence on the flats all morning. It was plenty cold.

In the afternoon I drove down to the ranch while Tom went to the lumber yard to pick up some material. My orders were to doctor the sick pen, look at the steers on the alfalfa, and check the water in three pastures. We all planned to quit early for the holiday. I doctored the sick pen and drove over to the alfalfa field, expecting to find no problems because this bunch of steers had been pretty healthy. I was hoping that I wouldn't find trouble because it was too danged cold to get ahorseback.

So naturally I found a problem. I noticed a nice black baldfaced steer that was passing blood. He didn't look sick and he was eating, but. . . . Then I found another that was lying down and didn't look so good.

I went back to Headquarters and saddled up Deuce, buttoned up my sheepskin collar, and rode out into the cold wind. I found the first sick one and drove him to a small corral we had made out of portable panels. As I neared the pen, Tom drove up in the flatbed pickup. The steer didn't want to go and ran north across a piece of electric fence wire that was left over from the stampede. The cattle had rubbed on it and dragged it out into the field.

Deuce had always been as silly as a goose about electric fences. I would guess that years ago, he walked into a hot fence and got shocked, and now, any time he sees an electric fence, he snorts, perks his ears, and starts prancing sideways. And that's what he did now. If he had just kept walking forward, he would have stepped over the wire with no trouble, but he started prancing sideways and got the wire snagged on his hind feet. That *really* woke him up!

He started losing his mind. He ran in a circle and got his front end caught up in the wire. He was running sideways and starting to buck. I decided to get down, in hopes I might be able to settle him down and walk him out of the wire. I held the reins and tried to calm him down, but he was scared and had lost his senses. He ran and kicked at the wire, and he ran towards *me*. Hey, I wanted to get away from him, but he kept coming back to me.

Then a new danger appeared. When Deuce moved, he dragged the wire with him, and it was getting around my ankles and snagging on my spurs. This was thin smooth wire. I couldn't even see the stuff, but I could hear it hissing on the ground and could feel it around my legs. Brother, I was getting worried. If I got tangled up in that wire with an insane horse, and if I lost control of that horse and he ran away, I could have been in very serious trouble. I might have been dragged or strangled.

I didn't know what to do. I was doing a kind of polka step to get the wire away from my feet. I thought about dropping the reins, leaving the horse, and just running away to get out of that invisible web of wire. But I didn't dare drop the reins on Deuce. As long as I had control of his head, I was safe. Also, I didn't know which way to run. The wire was everywhere by this time, in snarls and coils. Deuce had it around all four feet and I seemed to be right in the middle of it.

I got him stopped and tried to walk him out of the wire, but there was so much of it that I couldn't. Every time the wire touched him, he flinched and started running in circles again, wrapping me up in more wire.

Fellers, I was in a tight spot. Lucky for me, Tom had come into the field and suspected that something was wrong. He came roaring over in the pickup and asked what he should do. I told him to get some pliers and start cutting wire. He had us cut out in a couple of minutes. I don't know how it would have turned out if he hadn't been there. The thing that made it so dangerous was that Deuce wanted to run toward me.

Well, I still had sick cattle to take care of. I had to rope the second steer. When I started swinging my loop, the wind was blowing so hard that it plastered the loop on the back of my neck. I missed the first shot but connected on the second. I wasn't ashamed to miss in that wind.

December 4, 1979

Yesterday we cut seventy-four bulls. Ronnie Soviar (Tom's brother-in-law) and Clarence Herrington came to help. We didn't get started with the cutting until after lunch. Tom and I spent the morning doing chores, rounding up the cattle, and sorting off the bulls. With this late start, we found ourselves racing the sun, which is something we do a lot these short winter days. We worked quickly but at sundown we still had twenty or thirty bulls left. Tom wanted to get the work done, so we turned on all the corral lights and the headlights of a pickup. We finished at 7:00.

Clarence, Tom, and I did all the heeling, and for the first time ever, we all dallied. It is harder that way but safer and better, since the roper can dally up short and use the horse to help the men on the ground. The first time Tom heeled, he did badly. He handled his dallies well but he wasn't catching. This depressed him and he was in a gloomy mood. I told him, "Well, you're using that limp braided nylon rope and nobody could heel with it." He switched to Clarence's rope, which was an old well broke-in hard-lay nylon, and this rope changed his luck. He started hitting and double-hocking, heeling better than I had ever seen him do before. He was as happy as a kid on Christmas.

December 26, 1979

Not much excitement on the ranch these days. We have steers out on wheat and stalk fields on the flats, and we have to haul water and check fences every couple of days. Down on the creek, we're feeding alfalfa hay four days a week to the cows and a few yearlings. We feed about sixty bales a day, which is hard work.

The weather in December has been fair and mild, with only a few cold spells and little dabs of snow.

Not much cowboy work these days. We don't get in as much roping as we'd like.

January 17, 1980

The ranch work has slipped into the winter routine of feeding, building electric fence, and shifting cattle around. But the last two days we've had a little break from the ordinary.

Three days ago Lawrence bought forty-six yearling bulls and steers that averaged close to 500 pounds. Big ones. We kept them up in the corrals one day, branded them, and turned them out into the Home Pasture. Tom wanted to get them away from the corrals as soon as possible so we wouldn't have a bunch of sickness.

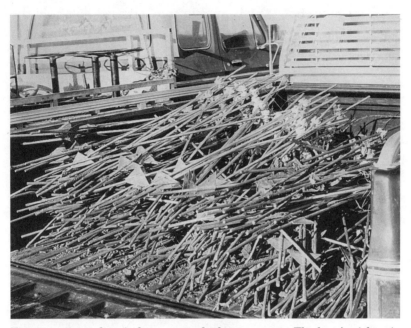

Time to put up electric fence around wheat pasture. The boss's pickup is filled with electric fence posts, while the spools of wire sit on the bed of Tom's pickup.

The next day they were scattered over the pasture, and Lawrence wanted to bunch them up and feed them so we could get a good count. He loaded some hay in the pickup and Tom and I saddled up and started pushing cattle down to the creek, where the boss was honking his horn. These cattle turned out to be a bunch of snakes, and Tom and I had trouble holding them. They were jumpy and wanted to run. They didn't have enough sense to go to the pickup. We drove them down close to the creek, almost to the feed ground, when a bunch split off and ran east.

Tom gave chase and brought them back, while I held the herd. Then a big Hereford left the herd and headed north. He weighed about 500 pounds and had big horns. I went after him and tried to turn him back to the herd. He dodged and kept going north. I followed him over to the east fence and began squeezing him against the fence with Calipso, thinking he would give up and go south. Instead, he made a razzoo at Calipso and would have gone under her belly if I hadn't turned off. I could have roped him easily, but I didn't want the boss to think I was playing cowboy with his livestock. I let him go.

When I joined Tom down by the creek, I told him what had happened. He said, "Let's go get him." I rode up the big draw on the east side of the pasture, while Tom loped up the other side of the draw. Up near the north side of the pasture, I found the bull. He was still running up the fenceline. This time, I didn't even try to turn him. I took down my rope and threw. The loop was right on target but it hit the top wire of the fence and glanced off. I built another and nailed him.

By the time I had dallied and jerked him around a bit, Tom came riding out of the draw, swinging a big hungry loop. He was using a new stiff nylon rope, and he laid down a perfect heel loop. When I saw the bull step into the loop with both feet, I spurred Calipso hard and took out the slack. I wanted to put him on the ground hard, since he had taken a shot at my mare with his horns.

The bull hit the ground. I turned Calipso to face him and noticed that Tom was slumped forward in the saddle. "Wait a minute," he said, "I'm hurt. I got my hand caught in the dally. I may have broken some fingers."

I held the bull down while Tom pulled off his glove. He told me later that he feared he had cut off one of his fingers and expected to find it in his glove. He was in bad pain, the kind that makes you sick and light-headed. His face went ashen and he broke out in a cold sweat. He got down and unbuttoned his coat and vest and lay on the ground. After a while, he got up and said that nothing was broken or cut off.

Meantime, the bull kicked out of the heel loop, jumped to his feet, and made a lunge at Tom. When he hit the end of my rope, he was only inches away from Tom, who gave him a boot in the nose. Then the bull whirled around and came after Calipso. I maneuvered her out of the way but she got the rope between her back legs, and when the slack went out of it, I had a little problem. She kicked at the rope and started bucking. I didn't want to cut bait and lose the bull, but I didn't want to get piled or injure Calipso either. I held on and talked Calipso out of a runaway, until she finally stepped over the rope.

The bull was still determined to go north and wouldn't drive, so I turned Calipso to the south and we dragged him. Tom came along behind and whipped him with his rope, and in a few minutes we had him trail broke. Down on the creek, Tom heeled him down, we got our ropes back, and turned him loose.

Tom's fingers were bruised and sprained, and today the middle finger was swollen up like a sausage link, but he'll be all right.

January 18, 1980

Today, Saturday, was supposed to be my day off. Tom told me yesterday that he might come up to the flats to rope and load a sick calf on wheat. I told him that if he was going to rope, I wanted to be there. So this morning he called and said he had two horses saddled, one for him and one for me, and he would pick me up in half an hour. I couldn't believe it. The sky was gray, a cold north wind was blowing, it was thirty degrees, and freezing rain was falling. But I had said that I would help.

We reached the Bryan place around 11:00. It was spitting rain and bitterly cold. We hit the saddles and rode through a bunch of steers that were humped up on the south side of the old barn. The rain turned into sleet. It was the hardest, heaviest sleet I had ever seen. It was like riding into buckshot. I could hardly force Calipso to face it, and it was stinging my cheeks and ears. We checked these steers and didn't find the one we wanted, so we rode north toward the pickup and trailer—into the wind and sleet. Calipso penned her ears back and tossed her head, and I thought she was going to buck in protest.

We loaded the horses and drove down the section-line road, which had turned to pure mud. It was only an eighth of a mile to the highway, yet the trailer wheels got so full of mud that they quit turning. Even the four-wheel-drive pickup wouldn't pull it. We had to unload the horses to lighten the load. While Tom drove, I rode Calipso and led Happy. It was very slow and there were times when it appeared that Tom was stuck, but at last we reached the highway.

We then drove to the southeast corner of the section where we found another bunch of steers. We spotted the sick one right away, humped up behind the windbreak, and rode toward him with our ropes ready. He would belong to whichever man got the first shot. If he went to the left, he was Tom's. If he went right, he was mine. He went right and ran halfway through the electric fence. When I made my throw, he was straddling it. If I had missed, he might have gotten out on the highway, which was beginning to glaze over with ice. That would have been a nightmare.

This wasn't the time to miss, and I didn't. I stuck it on him and took my dally. We loaded him into the trailer and went home.

When I was working up on the Beaver River, the cowboys had better sense than to ride in such miserable weather. Not these Ellzeys. They'll work in any kind of weather, no matter how foul.

February 7, 1980

Through the first half of January, we didn't have much cold weather, but around the twentieth the weather turned nasty. Since that time we have either had snow or cold, or else warm days and deep mud.

Two days ago a storm blew in from the north and we got five inches of snow. Yesterday morning Lawrence and I fed the cattle on the flats. It was around fourteen degrees, with a twenty to twenty-five-mile-per-hour wind. Bitter cold. I wore my warmest clothes. A month ago Tom ordered me a

John feeds hay in the snow, while five-year-old Scot Erickson steers the pickup.

pair of two-layered long johns from L. L. Bean. The outside layer contains about forty percent wool. They are superior to cotton-blend long johns and I intend to buy another pair.

I have also solved the problem of cold feet. I ordered a pair of felt-lined snow boots out of the Sears catalog. I knew some cowboys up on the Beaver River who wore them and said they were good, so I thought I would try them. They're wonderful. Not once have I had cold feet in these boots, and I have worn them in mud, snow, and extreme cold. Both the long johns and the snow boots have one shortcoming: if the weather warms up or if you go into a warm house, you'd better get out of them.

Well, two days ago Tom, Lawrence, and I were up on the Bryan place on the Oklahoma state line. Lawrence had noticed a bloated heifer and wanted to take her home. We found her and two more with scours. Tom took first shot on the bloater. Happy gave him good position and he nailed her on the first loop, but he was using his new rope, which was still rather stiff, and he missed his dally. The heifer took his rope away from him.

In the midst of all this, I was spurring Calipso and moving up for a throw. This was not easily done, since the heifer was dragging Tom's rope. I made a pretty shot and fitted it around her horns. We loaded her into the trailer and went looking for the next one. Tom located her, cut her away from the bunch, gave chase, and one-looped her with a long throw, and this time he got his dallies laid around the horn.

He gave me the next heifer and I had a hard time with her. The field was muddy and the footing was bad. Instead of running straight out and giving me my favorite shot, the heifer ran in circles and dodged. I chased and waited for a good shot and finally took what I could get. I made a poor throw but managed to snag a hind leg, which got the job done.

It was a good day. We didn't miss a loop.

February 16, 1980

We have had a long spell of winter weather and the cattle on wheat have not done well. Since the middle of January they have been walking on snow, ice, frozen ground, or mud.

Around the water tanks you can see blood on the ground from their feet.

We have spent much of the time this last month just trying to hold things together—hauling alfalfa hay up to the flats and feeding the ranch and doctoring sick cattle. We have accomplished almost nothing else. It has been hard work. We all go home at night exhausted.

Last week Tom complained about nausea and dizziness. He finally took the afternoon off and went to bed.

February 24, 1980

My usual morning routine is to rise at 5:00, write until 7:45, say hello to Kris and the kids, hard-boil two eggs, put them into my vest pocket, and drive to the ranch. Sometimes I eat the eggs on the way and sometimes I wait until later in the morning to eat them.

Two days ago, when I arrived at the ranch, Tom had the horses in the corral and wanted to round up the Home Pasture. I didn't have time to eat my eggs. We saddled up and rounded the pasture and penned them with no trouble. But then we noticed a steer down by the creek. Somehow we had missed him. We left the corral and went after him. It was clear that he was a troublemaker. He made a dash for the creek and Tom cut him off. Denied that escape, he made a dash to the east. I saw his move and turned Calipso to head him. She went into a gallop, but as she turned, she lost her footing on the frozen ground and fell.

I didn't see it coming. Suddenly it was there, a wreck. I was almost on the ground when I thought, "Get out of the stirrups and roll." I did. I hit several feet away from Calipso and she didn't roll over on me. Nothing was broken but those two eggs in my vest pocket—and they weren't quite hard-boiled. What a mess!

Tom saw me on the ground and asked if I was hurt. "I'm all right. Go get the steer." Tom gave chase, and as soon as I could get aboard, I was behind him.

Tom missed three shots and was fuming mad at himself. He is trying to change from roping hard-and-fast to dally roping, and he's having trouble making all those changes at once: horse, throw, slack, coils, and dally. I sympathize because I've gone through the same problems. Actually, his throws weren't bad. He was close on all three of them . . . but close doesn't count in the pasture. I caught the steer but got a front leg in the loop.

Later, when we cut bulls in the corral, Tom redeemed himself with a good exhibition of heeling. He was delivering the loop well, getting it under the cattle, and coming up with double-hocks. He dallied on every one. I was using my over-the-hip shot and didn't have much success.

March 7, 1980

Yesterday morning Tom and I loaded the horses into the sixteen-foot trailer and drove up to the flats. We put out some hay and checked several bunches of steers. After lunch, we took up four miles of electric fence, wire and posts. Dull work. I got blisters from walking. Around 5:30 we quit that and took the horses over to the Bryan Place. We knew of two strays and a bloater that we needed to rope and load. We saw the first one, a big Hereford steer that weighed 600–625 pounds. We tightened our cinches and rode toward him.

Tom got within twenty-five feet of him without getting him out of a walk. He made a long throw, just in case he might connect. Tom's range is much longer than mine and he often makes those long shots that I couldn't make. But this time he missed and the steer started running. Tom told me to take him.

I spurred Calipso and off we went. The steer ran straight out, which meant that he didn't have a chance against me. That's my shot, my meat and potatoes. I threw and stuck it on him. But for some reason Calipso slowed down before I could lay my dallies. I punched her with my spurs and she started bucking in a full gallop. I wasn't expecting that at all and she blew me out of the stirrups on the first or second jump. And it goes without saying that the steer ended up with my rope.

I knew I was gone and wasn't trying to stay aboard, but I couldn't get away from her. I landed crossways on the saddle. Then I was in front of her, *hanging onto her ears!* Then I hit the ground, which consisted of craters of dried mud that were as hard as rocks.

Tom yelled and asked if I was hurt. I said no and ran for Calipso, who had stopped nearby. I had to get my rope back.

Tom took three shots at the steer, and it was easy to see why he missed. Happy was bird-dogging the rope that the steer was dragging and didn't give Tom a decent shot. He threw a loop I'd never seen him use before, a sidearm "ocean wave."

At last we caught the steer and loaded him into the trailer. Then we went after a black steer that was a stray. Tom threw a good loop but missed. I did the same, then Tom connected with his next loop. Then we went after the third steer. Tom missed, but I hit on the first loop.

Well, I was a little sore from the adventure with Calipso. My left thigh had taken a pounding and I noticed a pain in my ribs, on the lower right side. I must have hit the saddlehorn. The ribs got worse. Two days after the wreck, I knew that I had cracked some ribs. It hurt me to cough or laugh. Sneezing was totally out of the question.

March 16, 1980

My ribs hurt all last week. They feel some better today. The weather is warming up, days into the seventies. We are getting winds with it. The wheat is starting to grow again, after it was frozen back in February. Cattle are doing well for the first time since the middle of January.

Yesterday the prime lending rate went up to eighteen-and-a-half percent, the highest in American history. Nobody knows what that might mean in the long run. Lawrence's cattle loan is set at two-and-a-half above prime. That means he's paying twenty percent interest. Twenty percent! That is ruinous. And to make matters worse, cattle prices are going down—probably because nobody can afford to buy cattle at that rate of interest.

One result of having good wheat pasture is that the cattle are bloating, especially the light steers on the Bryan East Place. Friday, Tom and I roped four bloaters and loaded them into the twenty-four-foot gooseneck trailer. Each of us caught two head. Tom roped better than I did. I caught both mine on the second loop. The wind was blowing hard and it bothered me.

Several days ago, down at the ranch, I had to ride out into the Home Pasture and bring in a steer that looked sick. Tom told me he was a troublemaker and to rope him if he gave me any problems. I wasn't worried and didn't even bother to put on my spurs. That was a dumb mistake. He gave me trouble and I missed four shots at him. He was a dodging calf. He wouldn't run straight, and I haven't come up with a solution to this problem. In a corral, I would have tried a hoolihan shot, but out in the pasture I didn't think a hoolihan would work.

Of course it would have helped if I had worn my spurs.

March 22, 1980

Last week, on one of my days off, Tom found a heifer up in the Northwest Pasture that had had trouble delivering her calf, and the calf seemed to have some kind of nerve or brain disorder. It couldn't stand up. It just lay on the ground, twitching. He decided to rope the cow and take her to the home corrals. He'd been hot with the rope for the past week or so and was feeling pretty sure of himself, but he missed a bunch of loops and was humiliated.

He called me that night and told me his troubles. He was feeling pretty blue. He enjoys humility about as much as I do. I said, "Tom, Stanley Barby told me once that cows are harder to rope than other kinds of stock. They run with their heads down. You have to turn them to the right and come in from the side."

He said he hadn't thought about that.

On Monday he had to rope a big bloated steer on the Price North Wheat Pasture. He missed three loops and then noticed that the steer was running with his head down. He remembered Stanley Barby's solution. On his next throw, he hazed the steer to the right and came in from the side with his loop. It worked.

Yesterday Tom and I were discussing special roping problems and I mentioned the steer that I missed four times last week. He was a dodger and I told Tom, "I just don't have a solution to a dodging calf." He observed that my standard head shot is aimed straight ahead. When I try to throw to the side, it breaks the rhythm and pendulum effect of the loop. He suggested I should aim for a spot to the right of the steer's head, then wait for the calf to turn into my line of fire.

At the time, I didn't think much of the idea, but the more I thought about it the better I liked it, until I concluded that it was a brilliant idea. Tom was right. He had analyzed my problem and had suggested the simplest solution.

✦ ✦ ✦

Tom and Hap line one out on wheat pasture. John and Calipso follow.

Yesterday Tom and Lawrence decided that we had better leave the farming alone and check the cattle on wheat. Tom had recently talked with a fellow who had found four dead steers on wheat: bloat. The wheat has begun to grow rapidly in this warm weather, and the new growth is potent enough to kill cattle.

So yesterday afternoon we trailered up to the Price North Place to check the steers. These are the biggest steers we have. They all weigh between 600 and 700 pounds. Up to now, we have had no trouble at all with them, no sickness or bloat. But yesterday we found a lot of them bloated, and we went to work.

Tom cut out a black baldie and got after him. He missed his first loop, I moved in and stuck a nice loop around his neck. I got ready to dally and nudged Calipso with my spurs, and blast her ornery soul, she started bucking again! And I had even taken the time to warm her up this time. When she did this to me a few weeks ago, I held onto my rope but neglected to stay in the saddle. This time, I gave my rope to the steer, then dug in and started hoeing on Miss Calipso's sides with my spurs. She was serious about the bucking but I put a ride on the hateful little wench and worked her over with the gut hooks. I wouldn't want her to make a habit of that.

I got her rode but lost a pair of fencing pliers that I'd been carrying in my chaps pocket. We went back later and found them.

Meanwhile, Tom went after my steer, who was now dragging my rope. He missed three shots and was boiling mad. What he didn't realize is that Happy cheats like a riverboat gambler when there's a dragging rope. He won't give Tom a decent shot. But at last Tom came up with two forefeet and threw the steer to the ground. I got my head rope back and we took the steer to the trailer. Since he was big, we used Happy to pull him in. That's one thing Hap does well. The rascal can pull.

We roped two more big steers. Tom was so rattled by his three misses that he couldn't catch a cold. I caught both steers—and Calipso had stopped trying to buck.

We loaded the horses and trailered over to the Price South Place to doctor some pinkeye. Tom decided to change ropes and use a new thirty-five-foot seven-sixteenths rope he bought in Amarillo last week. The one he had used on Price North was a five-eighths heeling rope, and I never did see how he could catch heads with it. It was too stiff, and had a kink in it besides.

He started catching with the new rope and one-looped three steers in a row. That improved his attitude.

We found several blind steers in this bunch, and they followed the typical pattern for blind cattle. They dodged and darted—not my kind of shot. But this time I tried Tom's idea of aiming to the right, and it worked. When you see that a calf is going to dodge, you just change your aim and wait for him to turn to the right. Tom had a good idea there.

By sundown we had roped ten head. We were bone tired and so were our horses. Today we will have to check the big steers again. When we checked them at sundown last evening, there were seven or eight that were starting to bloat.

Yesterday Lawrence was talking with a banker who had just returned from a banking convention. He said that bankers were not optimistic about the economy. They expect a recession. The outlook for the cattle market is not good. Lawrence had hoped to sell 200 feeder steers off wheat for eighty cents per pound or more. Right now, they would bring seventy cents, which would give him a loss of fifty dollars a head, and that doesn't even count the cost of gasoline, labor, and so forth.

He faces a tough decision. He can sell the steers and take his loss, or take them on to the feedlot and risk a bigger loss later, if the market doesn't turn around. The major problem, aside from the market, is the interest rate. The prime rate is up to nineteen percent and nobody can make a profit on borrowed money, no matter how hard they work or how well they manage their affairs.

We are facing some hard times. Lawrence said that my job was not in jeopardy, but he let me know that the future is uncertain—for all of us.

March 24, 1980

We have been watching the cattle closely for bloat. The worst place is Price North, where we keep the big steers. Tom and I looked at them Friday evening and found so many bloated that we ran them into the portable corrals and dry-lotted them for the night, with eight Poloxolene blocks.

We had planned to doctor pinkeye on Friday, but the wind was blowing so hard that we didn't. When we were riding through the Price North steers, I made some practice throws with my rope. The wind was blowing so hard that I couldn't even swing the loop. Lousy day. It's raining.

March 26, 1980

We had rain and blowing snow on Sunday. The snow didn't amount to much here, but north of us they got quite a lot of it. We got enough to make everything a muddy mess.

Yesterday, Tom brought the horses up to the flats and we rode through the wheat pasture cattle, checking for bloat. On the Price South Place, where the cattle have been very healthy, we found a dead steer. He must have died from rapid pneumonia during the snow. We found two steers that the others had been riding. One, a black baldie, was lame in his back legs. We roped him and loaded him in the trailer.

Tom says that these "rider" steers will get some kind of smell on them, perhaps caused by hot weather, and the others start mounting them. If left there, they can be ridden clear into the ground and crippled. Tom roped the other "rider" steer, then we cut out a Hereford that was bloated and I roped him.

After lunch, we moved over to the Bryan East Place and found more bloaters. By this time the wind had come up out of the south and it was strong enough to be a bother. Neither of us roped well. We caught three head, none on the first toss. Tom made his best throw of the day on the last steer, a small black baldie. Each of us had missed him twice. After my second miss, it occurred to me that he was running with his head down, and that I had been wasting loops on a target that just wasn't there.

I yelled at Tom, "Take him when he cuts to the right!" He fell in behind the steer, crowded him, and turned him to the right, then snagged him with a perfect throw. That's an easy shot for Tom.

We have taken twenty bloaters back to the ranch and tagged their ears to identify them as bloaters. Last year the Ellzeys lost fifteen head to bloat. We haven't lost one to it this year, and Tom and I are proud of that record.

Last spring I bought a medium-lay Billy Leach rope from Kerry Cox, up in the Barby country. I used it on the Beaver River last spring and finally gave it up because it was too stiff. I have been carrying an old medium-lay nylon that I bought several years ago. It has softened up and has become a good heading rope, but I have had a lot of trouble heeling with it. It won't stand up. Last week, after I did a poor job of heeling some pinkeyes, I decided to try the Billy Leach rope again. It has limbered up and it's about right for a pasture rope, soft enough for heads and stiff enough for heels.

My ribs still hurt. I can't sleep on my right side.

March 27, 1980

Wednesday evening, Tom and I quit work early, around 6:00 P.M. I went home and waited for my friend Marc Simmons, an author and historian from New Mexico, to arrive for a visit. Tom was eating supper at the Ellzeys' house in town when Lawrence came in from hauling water. He had seen a badly bloated steer on the Bryan East Place and was afraid it might die before morning.

Well, all our horses and ropes were down at the ranch. Lawrence called me at home and asked if I had a rope at the house. I said no, then remembered an old heeling rope out in the garage.

Would I care to go out to Bryan East and help them rope the steer out of the back of the pickup? I hated to miss Marc when he arrived, but duty called. Just then, Marc pulled into the driveway. When the Ellzeys arrived a few minutes later, we all piled into the pickup and headed for the country.

It was getting dark by the time we reached the field, but we found the steer right away. He was puffed up like a toad. Tom and I got in the back of the pickup. I built a loop in the rope, which was awfully stiff for a heading rope.

I stood up in the back, on the right side, and Tom held onto my coat tail to keep me from falling out. Lawrence drove toward the steer. I made a long throw and missed. I made another long throw and missed again. By then, I had figured out that in holding onto my coat, Tom was binding my throwing arm, so I asked him to hold my belt instead.

Lawrence maneuvered around the steer and got him moving in a circle. I knew that my shot would find him turning to the right and that it would be long. You don't get close shots out of a pickup, I discovered. Also, I would have to allow for the wind, which was blowing pretty hard out of the northeast.

I threw and the loop dropped around his neck. I jumped out and dallied the rope around the hitch ball on the back bumper. Tom walked down the rope and got him under control. Then Lawrence opened Tom's big pocket knife and performed "pasture surgery" on the steer: slipped the blade of the knife into a certain spot just to the left of the backbone.

We could hear the gas hissing through the hole. This made the steer feel much better and harder to handle, and Tom had a hard time getting the rope off. It was rather a gross affair, but it saved the steer's life.

The next morning, Marc left for Kansas and I hauled two loads of water to cattle on wheat. By 10:30, when Tom arrived with horses, it was getting cold.

We looked at the steers on Bryan East and found three bloaters. By 11:00 it was raining hard—on ground that was already muddy. We didn't know what to do with the bloaters. Roping in the rain and mud was out of the question. Even if we caught one, what could we do with him? In rain and mud, the steer has all the advantages, the cowboy none.

Then we rode upon the steer we had fixed the night before. He was puffed up again. We had to do something with him or he would die. We were pretty sure we couldn't get the stock trailer into the field, and we weren't sure we could rope him anyway. Tom decided to quit for lunch and come back later. The weather couldn't get worse, and it might get better. We returned three hours later. The rain had stopped, but as soon as we got ahorseback, it started up again. We rode through all 125 steers on Bryan East and found ten or twelve bloaters. Our horses were bogging to their hocks on every step. My gloves and chaps were soaked.

We drove about fifty head, including all the bloaters, into an old wire corral in the southeast corner of the field. I doubt that we could have backed a trailer in to load the bloaters. It was far too muddy, and getting worse all the time. But at least we could dry-lot them and keep them off the wheat.

I was cold, wet, and miserable. Tom tried to cheer us both up by singing cowboy songs, including Willie Nelson's "Mommas, Don't Let Your Babies Grow Up to Be Cowboys." Those words summed up my feelings exactly. I was wet from head to toe, and I hate to work when I'm wet. I could hardly see because my glasses were dripping rain water. My boots were so covered with gumbo mud that I didn't even try to put them into the stirrups.

Tom is wet, cold, and miserable, penning wheat pasture cattle.

When we had penned the Bryan steers, we rode through the steers on Price North. We found one bloater and dry-lotted him in the portable corrals on the north side of the field. By this time the rain had quit and a crack of blue had appeared in the sky. But there were still a lot of gray, low clouds around. It was an unstable sky. Amarillo radio had a tornado warning out for the Panhandle, while in Liberal, Kansas, radio was predicting . . . *snow*?

I was cold, wet, and in a foul mood.

Next, we headed for Price South. Tom drove the red four-wheel drive with the stock trailer behind, and I drove the blue four-wheel drive. We figured we had better take both in case we got Tom's rig stuck.

The road to Price South had a good caliche top most of the way, but the last half-mile was deep mud. We stopped and talked it over. Should we leave the trailer on the caliche and ride horseback to the field, or try to pull the trailer all the way? We decided it would be smarter to leave the rig on the caliche, but there was a problem with this. If we found a bad bloater, we would have to rope him and load him into the trailer. There were no pens of any kind on Price South. We were down to horses and ropes.

We decided to drive to the field with the pickup and trailer. The sun had come out and we thought the road might start to dry a bit. We drove a hundred yards and Tom stopped. He said the trailer wheels had balled up in the mud and had quit turning. He thought we had better not go any farther, so we unloaded the horses and rode to the field.

By the time we got there, we noticed that the clouds were making up in the west again, and had changed to a dark blue color. Tom said it looked like a black hole. We knew we had better hurry, so we split up. I rode south through the muddy field and looked at a bunch on the south fence, while Tom rode through the main bunch on the north end.

The sun disappeared behind the clouds. A line of blue and gray clouds was moving toward us. I put Calipso into a lope. We still had to get the red pickup and trailer out of the mud, and that wasn't going to be any cinch, even if we didn't get rained on. I headed for the northwest corner as fast as Calipso could travel. Tom did the same. We could see a gray curtain of rain moving towards us from the southwest. It hit just as we reached the corner. We let down the electric fence and crossed our horses, and galloped down the road to the pickups.

It was raining hard now. The drops were big, cold, and mixed with pellets of ice. My black felt hat was already soaked up, and rainwater, colored with black dye, dripped off the brim.

We rode as hard as our poor horses could go through the mud, and discussed our next move as we went—over the din of rain, thunder, and horses galloping through deep mud. The strategy was pretty simple. We needed to get the heck out of there before the mud got any deeper. We loaded the horses and hooked a log chain onto the back end of the trailer. There was no chance of getting Tom's rig turned around in this mud. We would have to pull him backward to the caliche road.

The rain was coming down harder. I was freezing. My gloves and chaps were soaked and covered with mud. The lenses of my glasses were about as clear as wax paper.

We hooked the blue pickup onto the chain. I threw it into four-wheel drive, low range, and we started backing out. I was never sure this would work. Even with the two four-wheel-drive vehicles, we moved very slowly. Both pickups were spinning and throwing up balls of mud. It took us ten minutes to travel a hundred yards, but at last we reached the caliche.

As we were taking off the tow chain, Tom wondered aloud what we would have done if we had found a badly bloated steer. I had wondered that myself. It would have been a horrible wreck, I'm sure. In that kind of weather, your options shrink to almost nothing. You can't use a pickup and trailer, and you can hardly use a horse and rope.

What a day!

March 29, 1980

Yesterday was another day of misery. In mud that was ankle deep on our horses, we rounded up the steers on Bryan East and penned them. We had found several bloaters that morning. The mud in the corral was six to eight inches deep, a complete swamp. It took us most of the morning to do this simple job. Each steer had to be pushed and driven, and to get to each steer, I had to waste my mare's energy.

While we were out in the middle of this glop, I began to realize that the elements had rendered useless all the tools of our trade. We couldn't use pickups, trailers, or ropes, and it was almost to the point where we couldn't even use horses. We had worked our mounts in this stuff three days in a row, when every step they took sucked energy out of them.

Tom and I take pride in what we do, and to find ourselves so helpless is frustrating. After we have dragged ourselves through the mud for days and days, we begin to surrender to fatigue. We're tired, bone-weary, and it is hard for us to care what happens. To make matters worse, the radio is predicting more rain and snow for the weekend, and we have been hearing nothing but depressing economic news. Wheat is down to $3.04 a bushel, stocks are down, gold and silver are down, and worst of all, *cattle are down.*

As we plodded through the mud, I began to understand what a wicked and cruel business this wheat pasture deal is. In the first place, we had cattle bloating, even as they were shrinking and losing weight in the mud. We had only bad solutions. If we left them alone, they could die of bloat. If we penned them in a muddy corral, they would shrink and run the risk of getting pneumonia. They would have nothing to eat except whatever bales of hay we could *carry* to them through the mud. We can't even get a pickup load of hay into these fields.

Second, if we can believe the weather report, more rain and snow are on the way, which means that this horrible situation just might get worse before it gets better. Third, now that the fields have turned to swamps, the landowners are calling Tom and putting pressure on him to get the cattle off the fields, because the cattle are tromping their wheat into the ground.

It's a legitimate concern. What they don't understand is that we are straining ourselves, our horses, our equipment to the breaking point—just to keep the cattle alive from one day to the next. We would *love* to have all these steers off the wheat pastures, right now, today, this minute. But without a couple dozen National Guard helicopters, that isn't likely to happen.

The other day one of the landowners drove up in his clean pickup. Tom and I looked like German soldiers retreating from Moscow: soaked, covered with mud, wooden-eyed, exhausted. The landowner said he was just "looking the country over and checking the rain gauge." Yes, and wondering when we might get those steers off his wheat, although he didn't say so. He didn't understand. A man wearing clean dry clothes and sitting in a shiny pickup can't understand our plight. He can't understand that we haven't even been able to *look* at those cattle in four days, much less move them. For all we know, they might all be dead.

We are in a terrible mess. We've got over 500 head of cattle on wheat pasture. They are bloating. They are getting weak from walking in deep mud day after day. They can't find a dry spot to lie down and rest. We desperately need to move them onto grass somewhere, but there is no grass up here on the flats. Twenty miles of mud lie between us and the ranch.

Today is Saturday. It's supposed to be my day off, but I can't leave Tom with all this burden. Lawrence has gone to Houston for a meeting of the Federal Intermediate Credit Bureau. And God help us, it's snowing hard, big wet flakes that will make more mud.

Here's our situation today:.

Price North. Yesterday we penned these cattle because we saw several bloaters in the bunch. We're supposed to drive them to an eighty-acre patch of graze-out wheat as soon as possible, but we have no water tanks there. In the mud and snow, we will have to set a water tank and then try to haul water to it. And of course, the steers might start bloating again if we turn them out on the wheat.

Bryan East. We have 125 steers standing in a muddy pen. Some of them haven't watered in thirty-six hours. We had to pen them because of bloat. We're suppose to drive them to a patch of volunteer wheat, but before we can do that, we must build some electric fence. We can't get a pickup into the field.

Osborne South. We haven't even looked at these cattle in three days. We have no idea what troubles might be there, though this has been a trouble-free bunch of steers.

Bryan North. We haven't seen these fifty-two heifers in a week. We haven't had any bloat problems there yet, but who knows what they're doing now? The road is so bad, we can't get to them. We need to move these heifers off the wheat but we can't.

I have a pinched nerve in my back and my ribs still hurt. I am feeling a constant and deep fatigue—day after day of slogging through mud, lifting bales of hay, and then doing it all over again.

April 1, 1980

I made the previous entry Saturday morning, during my writing time. I was feeling pretty low, obviously. But the day wasn't as bad as I had expected, though it was no picnic either.

I drove to the ranch and Tom and I loaded fifty bales on the blue pickup. We hauled the horses up to the flats in the stock trailer, pulled by the red pickup. While we were in the corral saddling horses, a heavy snow was falling. Tom muttered, "Tomorrow's Sunday. Looks like I'll have to work." Then he looked toward the sky and yelled, "If God wants me to sing in the Methodist Church choir on Palm Sunday, he'd better do something about this dad-blasted weather!"

Later, as we rode through the mud and snow, he began singing "He's Got the Whole World in His Hands." I noted a certain irony in his tone, as though he had begun to suspect that God takes better care of shepherds and wise men than he does cowboys.

Being around Tom lifts my spirits. Hard times just make him stronger. And funnier. When he yelled that business about singing in the choir, I roared with laughter. It was the best—and maybe the first—laugh I'd had in weeks.

We drove through blowing snow and reached the flats around 10:30. Shortly after we arrived, we got the blue four-wheel-drive pickup stuck in a ditch. Then we found that the battery on the red four-wheel-drive was dead. We unloaded twenty bales off the back of the blue pickup and were able to get it out of the ditch. Then we used Blue to pull Red and get it started.

We built some electric fence on Bryan, turned 125 steers out of the corral, and drove them onto some graze-out wheat. Then we drove the Price North cattle to another patch of graze-out wheat. All day the wind flew thirty to forty miles per hour out of the north, and most of the time we faced either snow or sleet. The sleet, driven by the wind, stung our faces and hit us in the eyes, but it was better than rain. I hate working in the rain.

We moved a stock tank to the Price North bunch, then hauled water to them. It was nasty work. We never got around to checking the other three bunches of cattle, and I'm not even sure we could have reached them. The mud was terrible.

April 3, 1980

We've had some sunny weather. Thanks, Lord. On Monday
Tom and Lawrence were able to reach the heifers on Bryan
North, and hauled them back to the ranch.

On Tuesday we drove 300 smaller steers down to the
ranch, a distance of fifteen or twenty miles. Tom and
Lawrence debated about whether we should drive them or
haul them in trailers. Tom thought we should drive them. It
would be cheaper (no gas, no wear and tear on equipment)
and also quicker. Lawrence was worried that we wouldn't
have enough riders and that we wouldn't be able to keep the
steers off the farmers' wheat fields along the way. Tom won.

We had four hands ahorseback: Tom, Janet, Lawrence,
and me. We started on the Bryan East bunch at 7:15. At 8:00
we had them on the south end on the field and were ready to
drive them across the farm-to-market road, which is a black-
top highway with some traffic. A sharp wind was blowing
out of the north and gray winter clouds passed overhead,
but the sun was out and the weather forecast promised fair
weather. I wore my red cotton long johns. My ears and hands
were cold, but otherwise I stayed comfortable.

We pushed the 125 steers across the highway without
any problems, and started the drive south. After helping us
get the cattle across the highway at Bryan East, Lawrence
loaded Deuce into his stock trailer and drove ahead to check
for open gates and other problems. Janet was on Frisco, Tom
on Happy, and I on Calipso.

We drove this bunch five miles south and threw them in
with the 180 steers on Price South, which gave us our trail
herd of 305 steers.

Before we could continue the drive, however, we had to do something about a black baldface steer that was completely blind. On the long drive to the ranch, he would be nothing but trouble. Lawrence told us to rope him and load him in the trailer. Tom and I slipped into the herd and approached the steer. One of his eyes was shut and the other was a grotesque white ball, like the eye of the Ancient Mariner. Tom told me to take the first shot, and reminded me to be careful, since blind cattle can be unpredictable and dangerous. I knew that already, or thought I did.

The steer never knew I was in the herd with him and I was able to get within range before he ever got out of a walk. The shot that materialized was one of my favorites. He was off to my right, walking perpendicular to me. Instead of dipping the right side of my loop to pick up his head, which is easy for a righthanded roper, I had to dip the left side and turn the loop into a vertical plane. I had used that toss many times before and I knew I could make it work.

I stuck it on him, and Tom yelled, "Nice throw!"

But then the action started. When the steer felt the noose pull around his neck, he turned and ran away from me. He moved so suddenly that I had trouble getting my dallies. Then, when he hit the end of the rope, he leaped into the air and came running straight toward me.

Behind me, I heard Tom yell, "Watch him! Don't get yourself hurt."

Since the steer couldn't see me or anything else, he was reacting out of panic. I was surprised by his action, so I was a little slow in reacting. For a moment I thought I was in trouble. It appeared that he would either run under Calipso or jump into the saddle with me. I spurred the mare and we got out of the way.

From then on, I never took my eyes off him. He was completely unpredictable and liable to go anywhere. Any time slack came into the rope, I had to make sure that he didn't go under Calipso and that she didn't step over the rope. I decided that the safest way to handle him was to drag him or throw him to the ground, so I tripped him down. Tom followed my lead, jumped off his horse, ran to the steer, and held him down until Lawrence could bring the stock trailer. Then we loaded him.

I knew there was danger in roping blind cattle, but I guess I had never roped one that reacted exactly that way. Tom said he roped one several years ago that ran under his horse. He got bucked off, hung up in a stirrup, and dragged. That's why he was so nervous, watching me. He remembered the incident with Rusty.

We started out with the herd and drove them south. We had no trouble until we were passing through the Ellis land, when the steers smelled some lush green wheat and went to it. We couldn't stop them. They were hungry, and it took us forty-five minutes and a lot of yelling to get them past the wheat.

At noon we reached the farm-to-market road, several miles south of the old Wheatheart Feeders yard. Mary Frances Ellzey, Lawrence's wife, met us there with lunch. We let the herd graze in the ditches while we ate beef heart, rice, boiled turnips and carrots, and homemade cookies. Not bad eats for a trail drive.

After lunch, Janet left with Mary Frances, and the three of us started the herd down the highway. The motorists who passed us were friendly and courteous, which is not always the case. One lady in a Ford Pinto followed us for half an hour. I guess she just wanted to see a cattle drive.

By this time the steers were trail broke and had slowed to a walk, and Tom and I brought out our ropes and started heeling the stragglers. We heeled cattle for the next five hours, solid. We must have thrown five hundred loops apiece.

At the old Glascow Place, we turned south and started down into the Wolf Creek watershed. At 4:00 Mary Frances caught up with us, just before we entered Percy Powers' pasture. She had brought sandwiches and soda pop. The break revived our spirits. We were all getting saddle-weary and red-eyed from the dust.

We drove the herd through the Powers Pasture, and around 6:00 we pushed them into the Ellzey's Northwest Pasture and drove them to the windmill. Tom and I both commented on how good it felt to be back in buffalo grass country, away from the flats with all its mud and miseries. We held the steers on water until they had drunk and settled down. Then we left them and rode away. It had been a good cattle drive. The weather had held for us and we'd had few problems.

The next day, yesterday, the weather turned foul again: cloudy, sharp north wind. I went down to the ranch. Around 9:00, while Tom and I were loading hay into the blue pickup, the clouds cut loose. First came pea-sized hail, enough to cover the ground. This turned into sleet, then snow, then cold rain with thunder and lightning.

We finished loading the hay, then saddled our horses. When I put the bit into Calipso's mouth, she held her neck at a strange angle and staggered a few steps. I thought she was sick, but after walking her around the corral, I realized that she was putting on an act. Like the rest of us, she was sick of mud, rain, ice, and snow. Tom remarked, "Sometimes it isn't good to have a horse that's too smart."

We took the hay, horses, and two pickups to the flats, and drove through rain and snow. I could see the mud on the flats getting deeper, and on the radio I heard that Chemical Bank of New York had raised its prime lending rate to twenty percent, and that feeder steers had dropped to sixty cents a pound. A year ago they were worth ninety; a month ago eighty. Lawrence figured that if he had sold his 200 feeder steers yesterday, they would have lost $140 a head—a $28,000 loss for a winter of worry, misery, and hard work.

We spent the day slogging through deep mud on the flats, shifting two bunches of steers around to keep them from tromping out the wheat pasture. We had to build some electric fence, and since the fields were too boggy even for a four-wheel-drive pickup, we had to do it all afoot. The black mud collected on our overshoes until they were so heavy that we could hardly drag ourselves around.

Along about 4:00 in the afternoon, Tom and I were weary. We had walked a quarter-mile out into a muddy field to do some work on the electric fence. On our way back to the pickup, we were dragging along, slipping and sliding through the mud. Then I picked up the pace a bit and got ahead of Tom. He caught up with me and took the lead. Before long, we were in a walking race, swinging our arms and going as fast as we could. Neither of us would quit. We stayed neck and neck all the way. By the time we reached the pickup, we were exhausted and panting for breath.

"You fool!" Tom gasped.

"You're so competitive!" I gasped back.

We drove around to the north end of the field and Tom got out to test the fence. "I'll test it. You stay in the pickup and rest," he said.

"Oh no you don't. If you can get out and test the fence, so can I."

We both got out and waded through water a foot deep in the ditch.

"Erickson, you're crazy."

"I know, but I'm not tired."

"Neither am I."

Later, when we were in a more thoughtful mood, Tom said, "I don't mind all this hard work. I enjoy it. I wouldn't mind it if we had something to show for it, but when you work your tail off and still lose money, you can get bitter."

Around sundown, Lawrence and I were hauling water to the steers on the flats. He was feeling blue about the economy.

"Here I am, sixty-nine years old, and I'm still where I was in 1937, trying to keep from going broke. I don't know why anyone would go into the cattle business."

April 12, 1980

Last Thursday was a gorgeous spring day, with no wind and the temperature up around eighty. But of course we weren't ahorseback on such a day. We had to go up to the flats and take up electric fence.

Tom had some things to do at the ranch, so I went alone to the Burkhalter Place and started pulling electric fence posts. I had me a system worked out. I would drive along the fenceline and jump out while the pickup was still moving, jerk the post out of the ground, throw it into the back, chase down the pickup, and drive to the next post. I picked up two miles of posts in about an hour and a half.

Later, we rolled up the wire and moved up to the Ed Bryan Place, then to the Osborne South Place. We rolled up seven or eight miles of wire and quit at 7:00.

The next day a norther blew in and I had to feed the cattle at the ranch in a high wind. We have had a lot of wind this spring. It got cold yesterday, and last night the temperature dropped down to twenty-eight degrees. Yesterday snow fell in some parts of the Panhandle, though not here.

We have pulled all the light steers off wheat pasture and have 300 of them at the ranch on grass. We left 200 of the bigger steers on three patches of graze-out wheat. They have gained very little weight on wheat. They looked good until that cold wet spell in March, and that took the flesh off them. They may start gaining it back on the graze-out wheat.

The cattle market is in a confused state. One day the futures go up to the limit. The next day they are down to the limit. Last week, on the same day, I heard a news report that said retailers had cut their beef prices by twenty to thirty cents a pound, then the USDA was predicting higher beef prices in months to come. Why would beef be going up when the cash price for feeder steers is down around sixty cents a pound, thirty cents lower than last year?

April 16, 1980

Yesterday was a genuine spring day, warm and still. You could almost see the grass jumping out along the creek. The elms are showing buds and the cottonwoods are starting to leaf out.

April 21, 1980

We've had several beautiful days in a row. The country is greening up and budding out.

One day last week I was working with Lawrence. It was a cold, miserable, windy day and we had just finished loading the pickup with hay. He complained about aches in his arms and legs.

I said, "Boss, I've heard that those are two of the early warning signs of gonorrhea."

He howled with laughter.

April 25, 1980

One day last week, Tom and I were up on the flats, taking up electric fence. He grabbed hold of a wire that he thought was grounded out. It wasn't and the 110-volt current almost knocked him down. His whole body jumped, and then he yelled some really inspired profanity.

This is Saturday. Last Wednesday night a big storm moved through and we got 2.7 inches of rain in town. Once again, the cattle on wheat were living in a swamp. The whole county was soaked and standing water. On Thursday the sky was leaden with low, boiling clouds, and we got a slow cold rain all day. In the afternoon Tom and I had to fence off one end of the Price South Place and drive ninety-seven steers on it and feed them alfalfa hay. It was muddy, miserable work.

Yesterday afternoon was cold (thirty-nine degrees), windy (gusts up to thirty-five miles per hour), and rainy. At noon we got a call at the ranch, with the good news that we had cattle out on the flats. We saddled up our horses, trailered up to the flats, and rode through mud six inches deep.

Here lies one huge difference between a cow-calf operation and a steer operation. With cows, you can wait for decent weather. With steers, you put on your slicker, grit your teeth, and get ahorseback. Your problems are most likely to come in the foulest weather.

And to make matters worse, we had just heard the news about the failed attempt by American marines to rescue the hostages in Iran. Very depressing.

Last week I encountered a new roping problem. Tom was in the horse pasture, putting out hay for the horses and five heavy heifers. I was on Calipso and rode across the creek to drive the cattle over to where Tom was putting out the hay. I found one of the heifers lying down, in the process of trying to deliver a calf. She was on the south side of the creek and I rode to her. She wasn't moving and I couldn't tell whether she was dead or alive.

When I drew close, I saw that both the heifer and her half-delivered calf were alive. The calf had hung up at the hips and couldn't get out. I yelled this information to Tom, and suggested that we had better pull the calf in the pasture rather than try to drive the heifer to the corral. Tom came running across the creek, and when the heifer jumped to her feet, he yelled, "You'd better rope her."

I rode toward her and began swinging my loop. That's when I noticed the technical problem. If I pursued her from behind, in the usual manner, the calf might fall out of her birth canal and Calipso might step on it and kill it. Yet I had to get a rope on her soon, else the calf would die inside her.

I decided not to give chase in the usual manner. I rode up on her left side and made a very long throw, in hopes that I might come up with something—head, horns, a front leg, a hind leg, just anything. I missed everything, but then the calf came unstuck and hit the ground, so it all worked out for the best.

May 1, 1980

Yesterday was another day of mud and misery. Last week we got over three inches of rain up on the flats, and yesterday morning it was at it again, a slow sizzling rain. It began to pick up and rain seriously around 9:00. Lawrence and I were up on the flats and had to load up the portable corral panels which were standing in a low spot full of water. We didn't have any slickers because we had left them in the blue pickup down at the ranch.

Our main job for the day was to load up 110 head of big steers on the Price South Place and haul them to the feedlot. Lawrence had hoped to sell them and get a price of seventy cents a pound. At that price, he would have lost money on them, but right now that price looks good. But he couldn't even get a bid close to that, so he's going to take them to the feedlot.

It was so muddy that we couldn't pull our stock trailers down the road to the Price Place, even with the four-wheel-drive pickups pulling them. So we set up the portable pens at the end of a caliche road, a mile north of the field. We had to build them right in the middle of the road because that's the only way we could reach them with the stock trailers.

Tom arrived with three horses and slickers. By then, the rain was coming down hard. We climbed into wet saddles and had to ride a mile to the south, into the wind and rain, just to reach the field we were to gather. Calipso was in a terrible humor and had a hump in her back for twenty minutes. She hates cold wet weather, and she has a peculiar way of walking that lets you know how she feels about it. It makes you think she's crippled, or that she's going to start bucking at any moment.

We found the steers humped up on the west end of the field, standing in mud up to their hocks and dripping water. We got them moving and drove them north toward the portable corral. They were so wet and pitiful that we didn't have any trouble driving them. We penned them in the corral, then pulled off our saddles and stuffed them into Tom's pickup. The horses would have to stand in the rain for several hours until we finished the loading and hauling.

We backed the twenty-four-foot gooseneck trailer up to the pens and started loading cattle. We had three trailers and loaded them all. Two were hooked up to the four-wheel-drive pickups, and we didn't have any trouble getting them out. But the third trailer was pulled by Lawrence's two-wheel-drive Chevy, and it had trouble in the mud. Tom and I had to push on the back end of the pickup to keep it straight. The road was so slick that we could change the angle of the pickup just by pushing.

We hauled the first three trailer-loads out before lunch. We were all drenched when we went to the Ellzeys' house for lunch. Our chaps were completely soaked up and useless, and we had to remove our jeans and hang them near a bathroom heater while we ate. Tom and I had to wear Lawrence's pants for an hour. They had four inches of slack in the waist, but at least they were dry.

We hauled cattle all afternoon. The rain quit around 3:00. The ground inside our little corral had turned to pure muck. It was the color and consistency of half-melted chocolate ice cream, and every time the cattle moved, they made a slurp-slurp sound and threw up a spray of mud. After three trips with all three trailers, we got them hauled, and by 7:00 that evening we had loaded up the portable corral panels and the horses. At last, we had no cattle on wheat pasture!

This has been a terrible year for wheat pasture cattle. Since the end of January we have had one wet spell on top of another. The cattle lost most of the weight they had gained in the fall, and cattle prices have fallen steadily.

May 4, 1980

Two days ago, on Friday, we rounded up 240 steers out of
the Home Pasture and penned them. These were steers we
brought home from the flats and which needed to get dis-
tributed in pastures over the ranch. The corrals were
swampy. It would be incorrect to say that they were "muddy,"
because what we walked through was not mere mud. It was
animal manure that had dried and then become saturated
with water. It lay four to six inches deep, was very soft, and
gave off a terrible sulphurous odor.

We sorted the cattle for four hours, dividing them into
four bunches. While Lawrence hauled the small end to the
West Pasture in the big gooseneck, Tom and I drove the big
end, a hundred head of steers, over to the Lower Section
East Pasture, about four miles east of Headquarters.

We started out at 6:00 in the evening. The steers were
gentle and easy to handle. We had driven some of them down
from the flats and they were trail-broke. As usual, Tom and
I had our ropes down and were heeling along the way.

Happy was sick with distemper, so Tom was riding Frisco,
a small sorrel gelding with a short gait and a nervous dispo-
sition. Along about 7:00 we were approaching the gate into
the Lower Section East. Tom was riding down a hill into a
draw. All at once Frisco stepped into a big hole and went
down as though he'd been shot. He didn't just stumble. He
went all the way to the ground.

Tom never saw it coming. He had just enough time to get
his feet out of the stirrups, but not enough to roll or soften
the fall. He hit the ground on his right shoulder, and Frisco

had one of Tom's legs pinned under him. I was about fifty feet away and saw the whole thing. Tom's first reaction was anger. He swore at himself for taking such a hard fall. Then he said he was hurt. Something had popped in his shoulder and he thought he had broken a bone.

My first first response was to go to Frisco, not to Tom. Frisco had wallowed to his feet and was moving away to the east. I reasoned that if Tom was hurt, he would need his horse to get out of there. I also knew that Frisco was hard to catch—one of his least endearing qualities. He would run when you wanted to catch him, in a corral or out in the pas-

LZ ranch horses, clockwise from left: Frisco, Button, Happy, Calipso, Lightning. The saddle shed is shown at the left. Tom Ellzey (L) and Jeff Knighton (R).

ture. He had done this to me many times when I had tried to bridle him, and it had made me mad every time.

I rode toward Frisco in a trot. I made no sudden moves and didn't raise my voice. I felt the pressure of the situation, but I knew that the more excitement I showed, the more likely it was that Frisco would run away. I eased up to him and reached out for a rein, but I couldn't snag one. He kept moving away. Then I grabbed the horn on Tom's saddle, even though I was pretty sure that wouldn't do any good. I was right.

Well, that was enough of playing footsie with Frisco. I had a loop built in my rope. I swung it twice and let it fly. It hung on his left ear and didn't drop over his head, but I flipped it and fished the loop around his neck. When he turned to run, I dallied up.

As far as I knew, Frisco had never been roped before and I expected him to fight. I didn't care what he did. If he tried to fight me, I planned to choke him down. I'd never had much love for him anyway. He had dishonest eyes and a weaseling manner. I waited to see what he would do. He stopped in his tracks and followed me, and that was that.

Tom was on his feet and walking around by then, and he'd decided that he was okay, no broken bones. He climbed back into the saddle and we finished the drive. The next day he was very sore.

I have thought about this episode and about my reaction to it. When I saw what was happening, I should have been ready to rope the horse as soon as he got to his feet. Why? Because if Tom had gotten hung in the stirrups, I might have saved his life by catching the horse right away. I think Tom and I both should make this a habit. When we see the other man in trouble of any kind, *ride to him* with a loaded rope.

May 21, 1980

Rain and more rain. We have had at least four rains in the last week. During one of them, we hauled water to the Price South Place. That was fun, pulling a 1000-gallon water trailer down that muddy road. We used both four-wheel-drive pickups and barely made it.

On our way out, the blue pickup slid into a deep ditch and came to rest against a barbed-wire fence. We left the red pickup in the middle of the road while we studied the problem. When we tried to start Red, the battery was dead.

This somehow expressed the whole year. The blue pickup was stuck in the ditch. The red pickup had a dead battery and wouldn't start. And it was raining again.

We spent the next hour digging the blue pickup out of the ditch, in a soaking rain. At last we got it back on the road. Then we tried to pull Red to get it started, but the back wheels would not turn because of the slick mud.

Great. We would have to pull Red through a mile of mud until we made it to a caliche road, where perhaps the wheels would grab and the motor would turn over and the pickup would start. Off we went. I was driving Blue and pulling Tom in Red. I had the gas pedal to the floor and was throwing mud with all four wheels.

After we had gone about half a mile through this mess, I heard Tom's voice over the roar of the engine. I stopped and went back to see what was wrong. He had managed to get his pickup started. Also, his windshield was completely plastered with mud, and to see where he was driving, he'd had to stick his head out the window, and then he'd started getting his face plastered with mud.

We got a good laugh out of it. It's nice that we can laugh about something.

May 23, 1980

Last week all the Ellzeys went to Austin to attend Jill's graduation from the University of Texas. One afternoon while they were gone, I went down to the corral and started patching the roof on the saddle shed. Some of the old wooden shingles had blown off and I covered some of the bare spots with new shingles.

There was a two-year-old stud colt up in the corral named Chief. He had been running in a pasture with three mares, but we moved him because Lawrence didn't want him cavorting with the mares. We will geld him when the opportunity arises.

I got my tools and a bale of shingles out of the saddle shed and went to work on the roof. The shingles were heavy and I didn't bother to close the saddle shed door. After a bit, I noticed that the stud had disappeared. I looked around the corral and didn't see him. Then I noticed his tail showing in the saddle shed door.

The little dummy had walked through the narrow door and was now standing inside the shed, in a tiny space just barely large enough to contain him. We had eight or ten saddles in there, valued at anywhere from $400 to $1000 apiece, as well as all our spurs, bridles, bits, and chaps. I could hear him chewing on something, and I sincerely hoped it wasn't the boss's saddle. This colt was not broke or gentle. We had never worked with him at all, and he wasn't even halter broke. If I did anything to excite him, he might tear the whole place apart, and possibly injure himself. Since there was only one entrance to the shed, I couldn't get in front of him to back him out.

I didn't know what to do. It was almost quitting time and I sure couldn't leave while he was in there chewing up our equipment. I thought it over and decided there was only one thing I could do: go back up on the roof and continue working until he decided to (1) tear the shed apart, or (2) back himself out.

I did, and at last he backed out the door. Best of all, he didn't chew up any of our saddles. The boss need never know that I broke the first rule of ranch life: always shut gates and doors.

May 27, 1980

One day last week I drew the job of scooping wet manure out of the twenty-four-foot stock trailer. Since we had been hauling a lot of cattle recently, the floor was covered with three or four inches of it. I got a scoop and a shovel out of the machine shed and drove the trailer out into Home Pasture. Shortly after I had begun working, Lawrence drove up. Even though this was the lowest menial job on the ranch, he wasn't sure that I could handle it without some advice.

Later, I complained to Tom. "Your dad doesn't think I'm smart enough to shovel manure by myself."

He nodded. "I've wondered about that too."

May 30, 1980

Last week we had rain and more rain. The wind went to the southeast and stayed there, blowing in Gulf clouds and moisture. We had just hauled the big end of the steers back up to the wheat pasture, in hopes they might start gaining weight after the fields had dried out. But on Wednesday they were walking around in water and mud again, and we had to haul them back down to the ranch, this time for good. We spent all day hauling eighty-five head. We got the last bunch loaded into the trailers around 6:00, just as a big nasty rolling cloud moved in from the southwest. We unsaddled our horses and left them standing in the corral and started for the ranch.

We met the rain south of Perryton. It was a hard rain with some small hail. It rained an inch and a half, and several tornadoes were sighted west of town, near Farnsworth. Tulia got hit by a tornado that same afternoon.

Down at the ranch, the country is as green and lovely as a golf course. The cattle are getting fat on cheat grass and the buffalo grass is looking great up in the north pastures. We have moisture in the ground and should have a good grass year.

Tom has been trying to break his young mare, Bonnie, to ride. Yesterday he rode her out into the pasture for the first time. Before he climbed on her, I led her around the pasture on Deuce, to warm her up and get some of the kinks out of her back. Then Tom rode her around the corral for twenty minutes and put a light sweat on her. We decided it was time to take her out, and we went for a ride in the Home Pasture. She did well. She reined and stopped, and she didn't offer to buck.

June 3, 1980

Yesterday was spring roundup day on the LZ. Scottie (my son, who is six) and I went down early and got there around 7:30. Tom had rounded up all the horses and he and I started throwing on saddles. We saddled everything on the place that was fit to ride: Happy for John Ellzey; Popeye for Lawrence; Frisco for Tom; Cookie for Jill; Deuce for Nathan; Button for Kevin; Lightning for Scottie; Stormy for Jeff Knighton; and Calipso for me.

Next, we loaded the branding equipment into the blue pickup. Tom had his checklist on a clipboard and we checked everything twice. By 8:00 some of the neighbors began pulling in: Clarence Herrington, Danny Herrington, Paul Sammons, and Kent Courson. Clyde Herrington and Myron McCartor came later. Skip and Jack Ellzey joined us down at the Lower Section. We split the crew and gathered the Middle and Southeast Pastures, and penned them in the Four Corners corral. A brisk wind was blowing out of the northwest, and it was just a bit chilly at first. Later, it warmed up to a perfect day.

Lawrence and Clarence did the roping on the first bunch, which had a lot of big calves in it. Most of these had to be heeled, and it was good they were both mounted on big stout horses. Calipso would have had a hard time dragging those big ones.

John Ellzey and I roped the next bunch, and we went through them in a hurry. These were smaller calves and we were able to rope many of them by the heads. John Ellzey tied solid to the horn and threw mostly hoolihan loops, and he did very well. I dallied and did well too. I used my soft pasture rope and it was just right for the job. I missed several heel shots because the loop didn't stand up, but on the whole my heeling was pretty good. We kept the ground crew busy. When we finished this bunch, we turned them out into the Middle Pasture, mounted up, and rode to the Lower Section West.

Scottie rode with me on the pony Lightning, and this time out, I didn't lead the pony. I let Scot handle him by himself. At first he was afraid, but he soon learned that he could control the pony and he gained confidence. Before long, he was challenging the other riders to a horse race.

We gathered and penned the Lower Section bunch and stopped for lunch. The long table at the house was set for twenty people, and it was heaped with food: roast beef, creamed potatoes, corn, green beans, red beans, jello salad, cabbage slaw, pickles and relish, and hot bread. And, of course, big pitchers of iced tea. When we finished all this, the dishes were cleared away and out came three varieties of cake and five kinds of ice cream. We ate until we could hold no more, then we found places to lie down and take a twenty-minute rest. That little rest after lunch is an Ellzey tradition, a good one.

Then we went to the corral, started the branding fire, and went back to work. Tom and Uncle Jack Ellzey roped this bunch. Jack, who had just retired from the ministry, tied solid to the horn and threw a hoolihan loop. He made long shots and did well. He rode a sorrel mare named Babe. Tom rode Frisco, and he dallied. He got off to a slow start and switched from the stiff rope he uses in the pasture to one of mine which was softer. He began to hit. He made a lot of long throws and connected with most of them. He did a good job taking his dallies.

Frisco gave him a hard time, though. He is a nervous, hard-mouth horse, and he often worked against Tom. Tom lost his rope once, and got his hand scorched, because Frisco wouldn't move so that he could take his dallies. He also tried to buck several times. Tom had to expend a lot of energy just trying to control the horse, and it wore him out. He said he would never rope off Frisco again.

We turned the cattle out to pasture and went up to the house for more cake and ice cream, then we trailered our horses up to the Headquarters place to castrate a yearling stud colt. We had nine cowboys helping, and we had our hands full. The colt wasn't halter broke and we had a hard time getting him out of the corral. (Lawrence wanted to cut him on grass, away from the dust and germs in the corral.) To get him out, we had to put a rope under his tail, while three men tugged on the lead rope. Once we got him into the pasture, he almost dragged three of us over an embankment and into Wolf Creek. He was going up on his back legs and

(above) Roundup morning, overlooking the Wolf Creek valley and Lake Fryer. L–R, Nathan Ellzey, Scot Erickson, John Erickson, and Tom Ellzey.

(right) Mary Frances Ellzey (top left of photo) fed half the county at the LZ brandings, and it was always delicious.

pulling us toward the edge. We yelled for help and several men came at a run.

Lawrence has been cutting colts for many years, and he has his own special way of doing it. He rigged up a long soft cotton rope so that when we pulled on both ends at once, it would fold up the colt's legs and cause him to go down. When

(above) Bringing in the cattle in the Home Section pasture at spring branding. Foreground shows an excellent crop of Indian Paintbrush flowers. Background shows the confluence of Northup Creek and Wolf Creek.

(left) Lawrence Ellzey, on Happy, loads up a hoolihan loop at spring branding.

we got him on the ground, we put a catch rope on his front feet, with two men holding it. Then Lawrence stepped in and did the cutting.

It was a great branding day, and we all had fun. We only wished he'd had more cattle to work. It was the kind of day and the kind of experience that the LZ Ranch can provide.

All kinds of people were brought together for a day of work and fun. There was a job for everyone, young and old, boys and girls, men and women. The young and inexperienced had a chance to learn from the others. No one got in a hurry, got mad, or got hurt.

June 12, 1980

The past two days Tom and I have gone out and roped pink-eyed steers in the pasture. Most of this was done in rough country and under difficult conditions.

I wasn't pleased with my head roping, but I must admit that I didn't have many good shots. I like a straight-running calf at a distance of no more than ten feet. The steers we roped didn't run straight. They dodged and turned. They were often going up hills and down ravines, and the wind was blowing thirty miles per hour out of the southwest. That wind ruins my roping. I just can't throw hard enough to beat a strong wind. It doesn't seem to bother Tom as much. He has a stronger arm than I.

Anyway, I missed a lot of shots, but it was good practice for the Pasture Roping Contest next Saturday. Tom and I decided to enter, even though neither of us has ever roped in competition before.

We did some of our roping yesterday in the West Pasture, the roughest canyon pasture on the ranch, and the conditions were difficult. We were chasing steers through tall weeds, down canyons, over ruts and cow trails and rocks. On five head, I never once had the kind of shot I wanted, and I didn't one-loop a single steer. I guess I've gotten rusty over the winter months, but I must admit that roping in that country isn't easy.

Calipso was great. She followed the cattle and seemed to enjoy the chase. Tom is heeling well. If Calipso is fast enough to catch those Corriente steers at the contest tomorrow, we just might look respectable.

June 15, 1980

Yesterday morning I got up at 5:00, drove to the ranch at 5:30, and arrived at 6:00. I started doing chores to get ready for our trip to the Pasture Roping Contest on the LS Ranch west of Amarillo. We saddled and fed Happy and Calipso, loaded them up in the trailer, and left the ranch at 7:00. Going through Amarillo, we blew out a radiator hose. If it had happened anywhere else, we might have missed the roping, but the hose blew right in front of a Texaco station—with a parts store right across the street. We were on our way in twenty minutes.

West of Amarillo, the country changes abruptly from plains and rolling buffalo grass hills to reddish soil and rough ranch country, covered with mesquite trees and cholla cactus. When Tom and I saw all that thorny brush, we figured we might be in for a rough day. We had roped in rough country but never in brush. That cactus was everywhere, and it was as tall as a tree, standing six to eight feet high and covered with thorns.

The pasture roping contest. "We got one of 'em caught."

The roping was held in a pasture on the LS Ranch, about two miles off the Boys Ranch highway. We pulled in and parked amid a whole swarm of pickups and trailers, many of them with ranch names and brands on them: LS, Coldwater Cattle Co., Weymouth Ranch, and others. At the center of it all was a platform for the secretary, announcer, and timekeeper. Beside it was a holding pen made of portable corral panels. In the pen stood thirty-two head of lean Corriente steers, weighing around 500 pounds each. They reminded me of greyhounds.

Just to the south of the platform was a tent. Under the canvas were a dozen folding chairs and two stock tanks full of ice and cold beverages, soda pop in one and beer in the other. Many of the ropers were swigging beer when we got

there at 10:30, which amazed me. I couldn't imagine trying
to rope with a belly full of beer.

Tom and I checked in, then unloaded our horses and rode
around the pasture. While we were doing this, the Calcutta
was getting underway at the judges' stand. Some of the teams
went for as much as $200–300.

The pasture didn't look too bad to me. The first 100–200
yards in front of the chutes was solid ground, broken only by
a few deep cow paths. If a man could get his steer caught in
that area, he would do all right. But the farther the steer
ran, the heavier the brush became. If the steer went south,
he could get into some rough broken country. If he went north,
he would find some heavy mesquite. The ground itself would
not pose much of a problem, but the brush would.

At 12:00 the announcer called the ropers to get ready.
We were team number twelve out of sixty-four teams entered. I think most of the men came from the Amarillo area.
Some were cowboys on ranches along the Canadian River,
and others were team-ropers from town. Most of the horses
were big.

When the steers went out for the first time, they didn't
run hard. They had to be hazed out of the chute and they
walked or trotted out into the hundred-foot neutral zone.
Many of them stopped at the chalk score line and wouldn't
cross it. They had to be driven across. Then the flagman at
the line dropped his red flag and dropped the barrier rope.

The second steer out didn't run straight. When he crossed
the line and heard two horses thundering up behind him, he
cut south and ran through some pickups parked at the side.
The header chased him out of this area, scattering specta-

tors and evoking laughter and yells of delight from the ropers on the side. The steer ran back to the corral, with the header in hot pursuit, then he made a run down a line of corral panels. The header finally stuck a loop on him near some pickups north of the holding pens. Once roped, the steer started fighting, cut a big circle while the heeler followed him, and slammed into the side of a red pickup with New Mexico tags.

Men on horses, including me and Tom, scattered to get out of the way. Everyone was laughing and yelling, "Western, western!" The steer knocked a chrome strip off the pickup and left a dent in the side. The header pulled him out of the parking area and the heeler finally got him roped.

We were the twelfth team to rope, and by the time we came up, not one header had missed a throw. Some of the heelers had missed, but the headers had done very well. I was impressed. These ropers were good.

We drew a thin black steer. He walked out of the chute and had to be hazed across the line. When the flagman pulled the barrier rope, I stuck the spurs to Calipso and away we went. We gained rapidly on the steer, and much to my delight, he ran straight. I got behind him and waited for my shot. He did a little dodging and ran through some brush. Calipso stayed right on him.

When we reached a clearing in the brush, I saw my shot and threw. I laid it right on him, dallied, and turned off. Tom moved in for the heels. The steer was running in a circle at the end of my rope, crashing through mesquite and cactus. It was a tough place to heel, and Tom missed two shots. He was disgusted and angry with himself. If he had gotten double hocks on the first throw, we'd have had a respectable time, though it wouldn't have beaten some of the earlier times.

The contest was set up so that if you got no time on one of your three steers, you were out of the average, and at that point you were allowed only a total of two loops instead of three. The worst thing that could happen to a team was to get no time on the first steer. When that happened, you were donating your entry fee to someone else. That's what we'd done. Of course we were both nervous. We'd never roped in front of a crowd before. If we had been working alone in the pasture, maybe we would have done better.

After the first go-round, the contest stopped while the steers were brought up again and penned. When it resumed, the steers no longer walked out of the box, they came flying out, and the easy roping came to an end. The times grew longer and the action moved farther out into the brush.

By the time we came up for the second go-round, the temperature was up around a hundred degrees and the wind was gusting out of the southwest. Our second steer should have been entered in the Kentucky Derby. He charged out of the box and headed straight for the brush. I spurred hard out of the box and caught up with him all right, but he took evasive action by running from one mesquite tree to another. This old steer had done this before, it seemed to me. Calipso, trained to follow a running animal, fell in behind him and followed him into the brush. I had no chance to throw, since I was trying to keep from losing my head to mesquite limbs.

At one point, I saw a limb coming up in front of me. I ducked and lost both stirrups, and we plowed through the tree. When we finally came to a little clearing, I had the steer lined out. He was out of my range but I figured I'd better throw now. The loop hit the back of his neck and fell off. We had been out-run, out-smarted, and out-maneuvered by a wily Mexican steer who knew how to use the brush.

Our third steer was another sprinter. After roaring out of the box, he turned to the left, which was bad for me because Calipso has always been "right-headed." She doesn't turn as well to the left as to the right. The steer got a lead on me while I was trying to get the mare turned, and then the chase was on.

We got into some heavy brush. Calipso, who didn't know anything about this big nasty cactus, ran through several tree-sized bunches of it, and I could feel cactus spines in both my legs. The cactus was so tall that the mare picked up a six-inch hunk of cholla on her jaw. Well, we were out of the money and I didn't see any need to prolong the agony. I had had all of that brush I wanted, so I made another long throw and missed. I was ready to call it a day.

What did I learn from the contest? Well, I know now that Calipso doesn't have the speed to be a good arena horse. Those big Quarter Horses and Thoroughbreds can catch a Corriente and give the roper a decent shot. Calipso just doesn't have that kind of blazing speed out of the box. She's a wonderful all-around ranch horse, but she can't compete with those arena horses.

Second, my hat goes off to those arena ropers. They proved to me that they are the best, whether they are roping in an arena or out in the country. They have the horses and the skill to beat a ranch cowboy at his own game. It hurts my pride to admit that, but it's true. This contest placed the arena boys and the ranch cowboys in a fairly even contest. The arena ropers had the better horses and the advantage of practice, while the ranch cowboys had the advantage of riding horses that were accustomed to pasture work, brush, and rough country.

Superior horseflesh and training proved more important. I'm disappointed that the ranch cowboys didn't make a better showing, but we all got beat.

June 20, 1980

Tom told me a few stories from his side of the Pasture Roping Contest. While I was trying to catch the second steer, he hung his loop on a mesquite limb and almost got jerked out of the saddle. On the third steer, when we got into the bad brush, he and Happy were heading straight for a big cholla. The steer went to the right of it. Calipso and I went to the left. Happy couldn't decide which way to go, so he plowed right into the middle of it. Tom had cactus needles from his toes up to his shoulders. Then his loop hung on a branch of the cholla, and when he tried to jerk it off, it popped back and slapped Happy in the rump with a hunk of cactus.

I got a pinched nerve in my back out of that deal, and it has made me miserable all week. I worked in pain on Tuesday. I couldn't sit down and had to ride lying down in the back of the pickup. I ate lunch standing up. I felt so bad on Wednesday that I stayed in bed. I went to the chiropractor three times, and I'm feeling better now, but I still have some pain in my right hip and leg.

Glory comes at a terrible price.

July 9, 1980

The Ellzey Fourth of July picnic has come and gone for another year. It was a nice and festive occasion, as usual, with a big crowd of about 175 people of all ages. Kids were everywhere. It was a hot windy day, which detracted somewhat from the volleyball.

Around 6:00 someone spotted smoke on the north side of Wolf Creek. Thirty men dropped what they were doing and forded the creek and rushed up the wooded bank to fight the grass fire. Apparently someone had set off a bottle rocket and the wind carried it into the pasture. It burned an acre or two of grass before we got there. Lawrence had gunny sacks and a barrel of water already loaded in his pickup, and he crossed the creek at the low water crossing and met the men at the scene of the fire. It wasn't serious, but if the grass hadn't been a little green, it might have gotten away from us. The Wolf Creek Volunteer Fire Department showed up with its white four-wheel-drive truck and they hosed water on smoldering cow chips, after our bunch had beat out most of the flames.

The summer has been very hot since about the third week of June. Around Dallas and Wichita Falls they are recording record-breaking heat, as high as 115 degrees. We haven't had heat that bad but it has been bad enough. One day last week when we were pulling pipe out of a windmill, the temperature was 106.

Yesterday afternoon I rode the cow-calf pastures. Before I left ahorseback, Lawrence gave me my orders, something like this:

"If you find any bad pinkeye, drive the calf to the corrals and we'll bring him home in the trailer. Or I guess you could rope and doctor him in the pasture, but one man working by himself can get into trouble if he's not careful.

"Don't doctor anything unless it really needs it. You can hurt an animal in this heat. But if they've got bad pinkeye, I guess you'd better doctor it. If you find more than three bad eyes in one pasture, just leave them and we'll round up the pasture later on.

"Ride the pastures well, even if you only get to look at one pasture, and don't lose my tally book."

Lawrence has a way of giving an order that anticipates everything that could possibly happen or go wrong.

When I rode away from Headquarters, heading north to the Middle Pasture, I hoped that I wouldn't find any pinkeye. Pasture roping at 100 degrees is hard work, and it also bothers my back. But I found a steer in the Middle that was blind in one eye and needed attention, so I pulled down my rope. I tried to get an easy shot at him but he wouldn't give it to me. I finally had to dig Calipso with the spurs and go after him. I caught him on the second loop.

In the Southeast Pasture I found more pinkeye. I could have doctored four or five, but I took the two worst cases. One was a big steer that I couldn't flank down. I missed my head shot but slopped on a double-hocker, and that turned out to be the best way of working him anyway. I dragged him so that he was lying on the slope of a hill, where he had to struggle uphill to gain his feet. While Calipso held his heels, I jumped off and doctored his eyes.

I carried my pinkeye medicine in a small canvas bag that fitted on my belt. It had a zipper on the top, and it was perfect for the job. Tom bought it last winter. In the bag, I was able to carry eye patches, glue, two syringes, and medicine. The bag was never in my way when I was roping.

Last week Lawrence taught me how to make a good tie with a pigging string. The secret is to get the wraps tight on all three legs. That string is very handy for pasture work, and it makes doctoring pinkeye much easier for one man.

Calipso did a great job yesterday. She followed the cattle well and held the rope tight when I needed it. But I have noticed that she is getting high-headed and excited when I take down my rope. This started right after the Pasture Roping Contest, when I spurred her hard to catch those Corrientes.

July 9, 1980

Yesterday Jill, Nathan, and I rode over to Dutcher Creek and started gathering the pasture from the south. Tom rode Bonnie and entered the pasture from the north end. The plan called for us to meet near the middle, where we would put the heifers into another pasture and then drive them to the Lower Section corrals.

It happened that Tom, Jill, and I were all mounted on mares, and only when we entered the pasture did we realize that Tuerto, the one-eyed stud horse, was running in Dutcher Creek pasture. I wasn't much concerned about this because I had faced him before on Calipso and chased him off with my rope. But Jill wasn't carrying a rope.

We started the gather. Nate and I were on the west side of the creek and Jill was on the east side. About halfway through the gather everything was going fine. We had our cattle moving in the right direction. Then Tuerto came thundering out of nowhere, heading for me and Calipso. I took down my rope, built a loop, and galloped straight towards him, swinging my rope. He threw up his head and stomped his feet and gave me a stud horse screech, but he stayed away from me.

But then he saw Jill's mare Cookie, and off he went across the creek. I yelled a warning to Jill: "Watch out, here comes Tuerto!" I went on about my business but kept an eye on the stud. Jill took off her cap and tried to shoo him away, but that didn't do any good. He got behind Cookie and it appeared to me that he might try to climb on her while Jill was in the saddle. I told Nathan to take care of the cattle while I crossed the creek to help Jill.

She had been driving forty heifers and had reached a place in the pasture that was notorious for a particularly vicious type of cactus. This was not our usual prickly pear variety, with flat pedals, but a yellowish type that had round arms covered with long spikey thorns. The needles have a hooked end, and when they get into a horse, they are very painful. Horses hate that cactus.

Swinging my rope, I rode after Tuerto. Every time I chased him away from Cookie, he kept circling and coming back. He ran through the heifers and scattered them, and they stampeded south up the creek. I was getting concerned by this time. Tuerto wouldn't leave, even though I was beating him with my rope and chasing him around. I told Jill she had better arm herself with a stick and fight him off. She dismounted and started leading Cookie toward a dead cottonwood tree, about a hundred feet away.

While she headed for the tree, I tried to keep Tuerto away from Cookie. I was getting mad, since Tuerto had scattered our cattle, and I whipped him as hard as I could. I chased him around and around, through that bad cactus, and though I tried to steer Calipso around it, she got into some of it. It hurt her so much that she began bucking and trying to kick a piece of it off her hind leg. I dug into the saddle and hung on, for I had no intention of getting piled in that cactus.

While I was chasing Tuerto around, Jill got ahorseback again and rode south to regather the heifers. I tried to keep Tuerto from following her, but that was impossible. I could see that until we got him out of the pasture, we would never get the cattle gathered.

By the time I caught up with Jill and the heifers, Tom had ridden up and the two of them were holding the herd. Tuerto streaked past me, plunged into and across the creek, and the hateful thing ran through the heifers again, scattering them like chickens. Tom then made a wise decision. He told Jill to forget the cattle and ride Cookie to the nearest gate and lure Tuerto into the next pasture. She did, Tuerto followed, and we shut the gate on him. Otherwise, we never would have gotten the pasture gathered.

July 18, 1980

We are still in the grip of a bad hot spell. Temperatures around here last week were in the 100–104 range every day. Dallas has had twenty-six straight days over a hundred degrees, which has broken all records. The heat has been severe in many parts of the country, and the drought is causing cattle prices to tumble.

I must say that the heat hasn't really bothered me much. Oh, when I get home at night I am very tired and thirsty, but I'm not suffering. Our summers just aren't as severe as those in places south and east of us. Here, if we have any wind, you can get along all right, either by keeping your shirt wet or by stripping it off. At night the temperature goes down to sixty-five or seventy, whereas in Dallas or Tulsa it might not fall below eighty-five. I would find it hard to work in that kind of heat. All things considered, this is a pretty good climate.

Last week we got to spend quite a lot of time ahorseback. On Tuesday we rounded up the steers in the West Pasture. Jill, Tom, Nathan, and I were riding out of one of the canyons when we saw two grown coyotes and two pups. The adult coyotes were very interested in Tom's German Shepherd, Sadie, and they seemed to have little fear of us. The coyotes barked just like dogs and Sadie went into the canyon and engaged them in combat. Neither had a clear advantage and both sides decided to give up the fight. They growled and barked at each other for a while, and that was the end of it. But I was interested in the way the coyotes behaved. They arched their backs and bristled just like cats.

Later, while the others held herd, Tom and I roped and doctored three steers for pinkeye. I caught the first two with one loop each, and Tom caught the third with an extremely long throw. It was so long that he didn't have enough rope left to dally, and he lost his rope.

Two days later Tom roped his first calf off of Bonnie. It was a pretty stout black baldie that had pinkeye in one eye. I got down and, after much struggle, flanked the calf down in the bottom of a dried-up pond. I suggested to Tom that we put the rope on the heels but before we could get that done, the calf reached up with a back leg, gave me a good hard kick, and overpowered me.

I didn't want to lose Bonnie's first calf, so I dove and grabbed him around the neck. The old lake bottom was covered with nettles. The calf was stout enough to drag me through these stickers before I finally gave up the fight. I was covered with stickers! I figured that was my payment for letting the calf get away. We had to rope it again.

Yesterday was a sorting day. We rounded up the Home Pasture and spent all morning and part of the afternoon sorting steers in the heat, wind, and choking dust. We had over a hundred head and had to sort them six ways. It was a slow, boring, miserable job.

Around 5:00 Tom, Nate, and I drove thirty-one head of steers over to the Dutcher North Pasture, a two- or three-mile drive. Naturally, Tom and I had our ropes down and were playing with them. Tom was riding Bonnie and she was doing well. We drove the steers to water on Cottonwood Creek and were heading back home in an easy trot, when all at once Bonnie stumbled. She went down on her chest and tried to regain her feet.

I was riding beside Tom and slightly ahead of him, and I happened to be looking right at him when it happened. The mare couldn't pull herself out of the fall and did a *complete flip*. When Tom saw what was coming, he said "Oh God." His voice didn't show fear or anger. He just knew something bad was coming his way—a broken back or pelvis, crushed organs, a fractured skull.

I watched as the mare's rear end went up. Tom was still in the saddle. My mind yelled, "Kick out, kick out!" Bonnie went over on top of him and he just disappeared beneath her.

I thought of jumping out of the saddle but decided against it. It occurred to me that the mare might not be able to get up and that I might have to rope her and drag her off Tom, before she smashed the life out of him. Fortunately, she rolled clear and stood up, quivering. I dropped Calipso's reins and my rope and ran over to Tom, who had rolled over on his back and was groaning in pain.

I told him not to move. I feared that he had broken ribs and internal injuries. But I couldn't keep him down. He wanted *up*!

He struggled to his feet and groaned, "I'm in an ant den." When he said that, I stopped worrying about him. If his biggest concern was ant bites, he wasn't badly hurt.

He had some pain in his lower back, where the cantle of the saddle rolled over him, but that was about the extent of his injuries. Boy, he was lucky to come out of that one!

August 6, 1980

Last Friday five of us—me, Tom, Nathan, David Ellzey, and Jill—rounded up the Home Pasture. We had thirteen dry cows that we wanted to drive up to the north end and throw into the Middle Pasture. We pushed them off the creek and toward the county road, which had only recently been upgraded from caliche to pavement. Several of the cows were reluctant, but we kept pushing them and at last they all went across.

All but one horned cow. She cut back on us. Tom and I got after her and tried to push her across, but she kept breaking back and it became clear that she wasn't going to cross that pavement.

"Rope her!" yelled Tom. I was riding Calipso and I had never roped anything as big as a grown cow on her. I would have preferred not to. But I was closest to the cow, so I built a loop and stuck it on her. Tom rode up and pitched his loop over her horns. He held her on Happy while I switched my rope over to the left side, so that we could pull the cow with two horses. We spurred our mounts and pulled together and jerked the old cuss across the road.

We felt pretty good about that. He and I had suffered many humiliations at the hands of such cows, but this time we had won the battle.

August 7, 1980

Tom and I spent three days this week doing nothing but riding pastures, counting cattle, and treating pinkeye. The days were all up around a hundred degrees and the wind blew hard out of the southwest, which made roping difficult.

On Tuesday we roped two big steers in the northeast pasture and both of us had a hard time getting a noose on them. Later, as we talked it over to get to the problem, we realized that both steers had run with their heads down and our loops had not fallen over their necks. This has happened to us before, and for some reason we can't see it at the time it happens. You get the steer lined out and make what you think should be an easy shot. It lands on the back of his neck and you think you just didn't throw hard enough. You don't realize that he didn't give you a head to throw at. We have not found a good solution to this problem yet.

On Wednesday we rode the cow-calf pastures. We gathered the herd in a corner and roped the pinkeyes out. Tom is better at herd-roping than I am because he can throw farther. I did poorly and had a frustrating day. I didn't make one catch in the herd. I was taking long shots and the wind was causing my loop to float. Tom was the workhorse that day, catching six of the eight calves we doctored.

Yesterday, Thursday, we rode again. In the southeast pasture we doctored two small calves and had to catch them on the run, which is my kind of shot. I caught both, two calves with three loops. Later, we rode the Home Pasture and I one-looped a big steer. I was feeling mighty good but Tom was showing that tightness around the eyes and mouth that comes from a bad day. One reason he wasn't catching was that Happy cheated on him. Tom would get position on a calf and just as he got ready to throw, Happy would slow down or turn away from the rope.

In the late afternoon we rode the Northup Creek cane field and found several yearlings with pinkeye. Tom cut one out of the herd and gave chase, determined to make a better showing. He stuck the noose on and tried to dally. Happy turned away from the heifer. Tom missed his dally and lost his rope.

Boy, was he mad! He yelled and spurred old Hap and galloped after the heifer. He chased her around in a circle until he got right on top of her. He leaned out of the saddle and snatched the rope off the ground. On the next one he made a perfect run and got the heifer caught on the first loop. He took his dally and brought her to a stop. The heifer started moving to his right. Tom tried to turn Happy with the calf but Hap sulled and wouldn't move. As the heifer passed behind the horse, the rope began pulling Tom out of the saddle.

He kicked out of the stirrups and yelled, "John, I'm going to fall!" Sure enough, he hit the ground but held on to the rope. I threw my rope away and rode to him and told him to hand me his. He did and I managed to dally on the very end of it. Tom had lost his hat and glasses, and he was furious at Happy, as he should have been. The horse had been goldbricking all day, and on this last heifer, he had put Tom in a bad position. If Tom had been tied solid to the horn, it could have been a serious wreck.

John and Calipso after one on the flats.

Stretching one out on the flats. L–R, Calipso, Tom, John, Happy.

I was carrying an extra rope, so Tom took it and used it to heel the heifer. We bedded her down and doctored her eyes. Then we had to go back and look for his glasses.

This field had been planted to hay grazer and it was up knee-high. That made it hard to find something as small as a pair of glasses, but we located my rope where I had throw it down and we used it as a landmark. I knew about where I had been in relation to Tom when I had dropped it, and after a few minutes, I spotted the glasses in the dirt. Fortunately, our horses had not stepped on them.

We roped one more heifer and went to the house for a cold drink. It had been a productive three days. We had checked all the cattle on the ranch and doctored eighteen head for pinkeye.

August 16, 1980

Last week was cooler, with highs in the eighties and nineties. On Thursday we had a gentle rain that covered the whole area, 1.3 inches at the ranch. It was probably a result of Hurricane Allen.

Thursday afternoon, Jill and I rode out in the Lower Section East Pasture and gathered up five cows, four yearlings, and one bull. We drove them to the Lower Section corral. I was on Calipso and Jill rode Happy, using Lawrence's saddle. Since it was an easy job and a short ride, she didn't change the stirrups. They were set for Lawrence and they were too long for her.

As we funnelled the cattle into the pens, a steer calf broke away. He weighed around 300 pounds, was half-blind with pinkeye, and acted crazy. We got around him and tried to ease him into the pens, but he wouldn't even face the gate and broke away from us several more times.

I built a loop and when he broke again, I went after him. I couldn't get a decent shot. He ran around a tree and got a lead on me. Then he headed straight for the fence east of Skip Ellzey's house. I dropped off and hoped he would stop or turn, but he hit the fence at full speed. We opened a wire gate and went through into this little horse trap. Things were getting tense now. We didn't want to run the calf into Skip's yard, and we sure didn't want him to get into the trees and brush along the creek.

We eased him out of the horse trap and down the hogwire fence toward the corral gate. He kept breaking away but we kept pushing him east. I really didn't want to try to rope him on the run again because of all the trees in the area. We got him up to the gate and he broke away. Jill was closer to him than I. When the calf ran, Happy went with him and made a brilliant cuttinghorse move. Jill wasn't ready for it and since her stirrups were too long, she got spilled. She hit the ground *hard*. I heard it.

I saw the empty saddle and saw her on the ground. The calf ran toward me and I calculated that he would pass right in front of my mare. I would get one shot at him, and if I missed, we might be chasing him all afternoon. I threw, stuck in on his neck, and dallied up. Only then did I look over in Jill's direction to see how she was doing. She was still on the ground and appeared to be hurt.

By this time Lawrence had seen her and came at a run. She had hit the ground on her hip and head. It knocked the wind out of her and she wasn't sure how badly she was hurt. Lawrence took off his hat and fanned her face. I couldn't do anything because I had a half-blind calf on the string, so I dragged him into the corral, flanked him down, and tied him. Jill was all right, but quite sore in the hip and neck for several days.

August 21, 1980

The weather this past week has been fallish. The mornings are cool, the days not terribly hot (eighty-five to ninety-three degrees), and darkness is coming earlier. We got an inch and a half of rain at the ranch last week.

On Tuesday afternoon Lawrence, Nathan, Tom, and I trailered our horses over to the Dutcher cane field. We gathered the cattle in a corner and Tom and I roped and doctored two calves with pinkeye. Then Lawrence started cutting out some old cows and heifers he wanted to take to the Beaver sale. We noticed that clouds were building up in the south and southwest.

When the cutting was done, we discussed the situation: should we drive the culls back to headquarters and try to beat the storm, or park them in the Dutcher Horse Pasture for the night? We decided to drive the cattle back to Headquarters, a distance of two or three miles.

Tom and I started out with the little herd, while Lawrence and Nate loaded their horses into the trailer and went west to do something else. Lawrence said he would watch the clouds and come pick us up if the storm hit. Tom and I drove the cattle west on the Wolf Creek road. We had fences on both sides, so it was an easy job. We pushed them across the low water crossing at Dutchers. About a quarter-mile west of the crossing, we topped a little rise and could see the country up ahead.

The caprocks on the Parnell Ranch were disappearing behind a curtain of heavy rain, and it was moving our way. We tried to hurry the cattle. An old thin cow brought up the rear, and I was following her down the middle of the road. I popped her on the behind with my rope and she drifted over into the south ditch. I went with her and tried to drive her back onto the road.

The first sprinkles of rain hit us, and all of a sudden the old cow just disappeared. She had stepped into a deep hole, about six feet across and five feet deep, that had grown over with weeds and was invisible. She fell in and couldn't get out. I called Tom over and we studied the problem. We thought that Happy might be able to yank her out, so Tom pitched his loop over her horns and gave Hap the spurs. Happy got down and pulled, but the cow hardly moved at all. She was in too deep.

Just then we were hit by a sheet of rain that was driven by a powerful wind. Lightning popped all around us. Lawrence arrived just then with the pickup and trailer. Tom dropped his rope and left the cow where she was. In just a matter of seconds, we were both soaked to the bone. Holding onto our hats, we struggled to open the trailer gate in the wind, loaded the horses, and struggled again to close it.

That wind, we learned later, tore limbs off trees and blew bales of hay off the top of the haystack. The rain was so hard and cold that I could hardly catch my breath. We dived into the pickup and squeezed in with Lawrence and Nathan. Only minutes before, we had been sweating. Now Lawrence had the heater running full blast. I'll bet the temperature had dropped thirty degrees in a matter of minutes. The wind rocked the pickup and we could see nothing but rain out the windows.

Then, as suddenly as it had come, it passed. Still dripping, we got out and went to check the cow. The hole she had stepped into was catching runoff water from a culvert, and it was filling up fast. If we didn't jerk her out of there, she would drown.

Lawrence had been riding Popeye that day, and at 1300 pounds he was the biggest, stoutest horse on the ranch. We unloaded him and Happy out of the trailer and pulled the cow with both horses. Tom and I hit our ropes at the same time, and after several jerks, we dragged the old cow out and drove the herd the rest of the way to Headquarters.

September 6, 1980

Last week Tom and I rode pastures and doctored pinkeye, which was a welcome relief from tractor driving. In one day we doctored eleven head of stock, ranging from small calves to one ox that weighed about 650 pounds. Neither of us had a spectacular day, but we both did a respectable job.

Making medicine on roundup morning. Jeff Knighton, John Erickson, Tom Ellzey.

On Thursday we gathered 160 head of big steers out of three pastures and penned them in the Four Corners corral. We cut out ten head with pinkeye, and in the late afternoon we team-roped and doctored them in the wire pen. Janet, Tom's wife, was there to help. She kept the syringe full of medicine, a mixture of antibiotic and cortisone, and put glue on the eye patches.

While we were doing this job, Tom got himself in the derndest mess I ever saw. He head-roped a big 600-pound steer. It started running, Happy turned away from him (exactly the wrong move for a dally man), and Tom tried to take a fast dally to avoid losing his rope. I'm not sure exactly what happened next, but the result was that he got his glove caught in the dally and the rope half-hitched over the horn so that it wouldn't slip.

He didn't say a word, so I didn't know he was in trouble. He spurred Happy forward to put some slack in the rope while he fought to get his hand free. In the process, Happy stepped over the rope with his front feet. Still, Tom said nothing and I didn't know his hand was caught.

The steer ran around the pen and pulled the rope tight around Happy's front legs. He started snorting and bucking. I yelled for Tom to get off, but he couldn't move. His hand was still caught and the rope was winding around him and pinning him onto the saddle. That's when I knew we had a problem.

Happy bucked over to the hogwire fence, and he bucked hard enough to break one of Tom's spur straps. The bucking also jerked Tom's glove out of the dally, and he was able to jump out of the saddle and grab hold of the fence. The rope was still half-hitched to the saddle horn, which meant that Happy and the big steer were married. The loose coils of rope hissed under Happy's belly and legs. When the steer hit the end of the rope, a coil wrapped around both of Happy's back legs. He folded up and went down.

If either the horse or the steer had tried to struggle at this point, we could have witnessed a terrible carnage. But Happy couldn't do much, since he was double-hocked, and the steer had just about choked himself down. Both animals stopped fighting and Tom went to work trying to get the rope off his saddlehorn.

I stood by on Calipso, with a loop in my hands. If the steer had moved, I would have roped him. I really didn't know what else to do. The thought crossed my mind that I could jump down and cut the rope, but this was a brand new forty dollar nylon rope, and this was the first time Tom had ever used it. I wasn't going to cut it until he told me to.

Finally, he got his rope off the horn and we went back to work. Tom's hands were shaking and his thumb hurt. Next time I see something like this, I'm going to cut the rope, and never mind now much it cost. Tom could have gotten himself killed.

It bothered me that I was so calm about this. I have seen Tom in so many tight spots lately, all of which he got out of, that I have a tendency to stand back and wait. When those wrecks occur, you don't have time to watch. You need to act fast.

On the other hand, Tom always seems to get out of them.

September 7, 1980

Fall is in the air. The days are getting shorter and the mornings are fresh, cool, and damp. It still gets hot in the afternoons, but we don't have the oppressive heat we had a few weeks ago. Yesterday afternoon a little cloud passed over and lightning started a grass fire over on the Parnell Ranch, just east of our Home Pasture. We were working on a tractor and Tom smelled smoke. We dropped everything, loaded gunny sacks, water, and shovels, and went to the fire. Janet stayed at the house and alerted the neighbors up and down the creek.

The Wolf Creek Fire Department truck came at once and we had ten or twelve men on the fire line. We got control of it quickly, then spent two hours going back and putting out fence posts and cow chips.

September 13, 1980

Tom and I did a nifty piece of work the other day. We were prowling the Northup cane field, looking for pinkeye. Jill was with us. We came up one steer short on our count and had to ride down into the heavy timber along Northup Creek.

We heard a calf bawling in the timber, south of the creek, but we couldn't see him. Tom sent me over to check it out. I heard the bawling again but still couldn't see him. The undergrowth was so heavy that I left Calipso ground-tied and walked into the brush. I found a Hereford steer totally blind with pinkeye.

I drove him out of the timber afoot, then climbed on Calipso and headed him north, out of the creek bottom. Tom and Jill joined me and we pushed him toward the cane field. Driving him was hard, because he was blind and reacted to sounds. Tom and Jill got behind him and eased him toward the gate. I took up a position near the gate and built a loop. We wanted to get a rope on him immediately, to make sure he didn't run back down into the wooded bottom.

He came toward me and was almost within range when he heard Calipso swish her tail at a fly. He boogered. I knew I would get one shot only. I threw and dropped the loop around his neck. So far, so good, but when the loop pulled tight around his neck, he leaped into the fence and went through the wires.

Well, that was a mess. I had him roped, but we were on opposite sides of the barbed wire fence. Tom rode up and dismounted. He told me to give him the rope and he would get it through the wire and hand it to me on the other side.

Good idea, but the steer started fighting hard and got away, dragging my rope. Tom jumped into the saddle and we started after the steer. The closer we got to him, the faster he ran. I knew the steer was blind and couldn't see me, so I devised a plan. I galloped Calipso around the edge of the field, where the cane was grazed off, and got in front of him, then jumped out of the saddle and got in a straight line with him.

I stood still, making no sound that would cause him to change course. He ran straight to me and past me. I reached down and grabbed the rope, and when Tom rode by, I handed it to him. He dallied up and we finished the job.

We were proud of that piece of ranch work.

October 10, 1980

We are in some nice fall weather, with cool nights and warm days. We are in the process of receiving light cattle and getting them ready to go onto wheat pasture.

All at once we're having health problems in the steers, due in large part to the change in seasons. In the summer or winter, the difference between daytime and nighttime temperatures runs about thirty degrees, but in the fall that spread might be as much as forty or even fifty degrees. One day last week it got up to ninety-three degrees. A norther came through in the night and the temperature fell to forty-four. The cattle are getting their winter coats and during these hot days, they suffer from the heat, then get chilled at night. Humans are affected by this, too. A lot of people in town have colds.

We are trying to plant wheat, even though we've had no moisture since August. The dryland wheat is doing no good at all. This tractor driving is a pain in the neck. All of us hate it. It seems the tractors are always breaking down, one little problem after another. Tom gets the tractors running again and we carry on.

October 17, 1980

The other day I found a dead cow in the Dutcher cane field. She was lying along the west fence, bloated with her legs sticking out. When I approached her, I noticed that her rectum and privates were gone, leaving a round hole about eight inches in diameter. It was almost perfectly round.

The next thing I noticed was that she had no udder. The bag was gone but I saw no signs of cutting or chewing, as though the bag had never been there. I also noticed that her lips were missing and her tongue was gone.

I made the usual assumptions—that coyotes had picked on the carcass—but the next day I began to wonder if perhaps the cow had been mutilated. Something about the carcass and the missing parts had struck me as odd at the

time but I had supplied the answers with my own precon-
ceived notions.

I had read a lot about cattle mutilations in my livestock
papers. In 1974 or 1975, while I was working on the Crown
Ranch in Beaver County, Oklahoma, the *Record Stockman*
carried a number of stories about mutilations in New Mexico
and Colorado. Many of the carcasses found in those states
bore the same marks as the cow I had found: a "cored" rectum; missing tongue, lips, and udder, all of which appeared
to have been done with "surgical" precision. The mutilations
in New Mexico and Colorado involved hundreds of animals.
Ranchers were up in arms and attending meetings at night
to discuss courses of action. The Colorado Bureau of Investigation and the FBI were called in to find the culprits who,
everyone assumed, were "cultists" who used animal parts
for some exotic ceremonies.

What interests me about the mutilations is that, for several months, it was major front-page news. Then, suddenly,
all references to the subject disappeared. As far as I can
determine, no one, "cultist" or otherwise, was ever caught,
charged, or brought to trial. The mutilations stopped and so
did the news stories.

This is very puzzling to me. In my reading on the subject, I have learned that mutilations of cattle and horses have
occurred all over the United States and Canada, and perhaps even in Europe and Latin America. It has been going
on for years, has involved thousands or tens of thousands of
cases, yet no one has found an explanation for it. It is a mys-
tery of the first order. So why is there not an ongoing
investigation? I don't know. Why didn't I report my discov-

ery to the sheriff's department, or even mention it to the
boss? Everyone who is touched by cattle mutilations seems
anxious to ignore it, to "let sleeping dogs lie."

Was the cow I found actually mutilated? I can't be sure.
All I can say is that it struck me as odd, and I have seen
hundreds of dead animals out in the pasture, not one of which
I ever thought was out of the ordinary.

October 27, 1980

Last Sunday a norther blew in and put an end to the pretty
fall weather. It has been windy and cold for three days,
twenty-four degrees this morning. I went down to the ranch
on Sunday and cut up some bodark and chinaberry wood for
the stove.

We started running the light steers on the alfalfa field
last week, so that has become part of our routine, running
them on in the morning and moving them off in the evening.
We have the heavier steers, 130 or so, on corn stalk fields on
the flats. Our wheat on the ranch is planted but we are so
dry that it isn't doing much.

October 25 was the last day of Daylight Saving Time. We
weaned calves and sorted cows in the Four Corners corral
all day and I didn't get home until 9:30. Days are shorter
now, getting dark around 6:00.

November 8, 1980

For the past week or so we've been back to warm weather,
with highs up in the seventies and eighties. And no wind.

Beautiful Indian Summer weather. The cottonwoods and willows along the creek have finally turned yellow, and it is quite a spectacular sight. I don't know why the trees were so slow to turn this year. Maybe it had something to do with the dry weather.

We have about 200 head of light cattle on alfalfa, and we run them on and off every day. We have fenced off some wheat up on the flats and next week we will haul cattle and put them out. The only good wheat in the country is irrigated. Not much dryland wheat.

Yesterday, Tom, Lawrence, and I sorted about twenty-eight heifers out of the bunch on alfalfa and drove them to the Headquarters corrals. They were typical yearling heifers, flighty and nervous. We kept them together and had them near the pens. I rode to the corral to open the gate. I left Calipso ground-tied and she began walking toward some green grass nearby. One end of the rope, which I'd left coiled over the saddlehorn, fell to the ground. She stepped on it with her back legs, spooked and stampeded right through the middle of the heifers and scattered them. Tom and Lawrence rode hard and managed to hold them, but here came Calipso again. She ran through the middle of them, dragging the rope behind her.

The heifers were ready to quit the country by this time, and I was ready to wring Calipso's neck. She had never done anything like that before. She ran to the horse pasture gate and stopped. I jumped aboard and galloped out to help Tom and Lawrence. If we had had more than twenty-eight, we would have spilled them all over the country, but with three of us whipping and spurring, we were able to hold them together.

I don't know why Calipso was so goosey. Well . . . come to think of it, that same morning we had run through an electric fence and ridden over two rattlesnakes. That might have put her nerves on edge.

November 16, 1980

A norther moved in around 9:00 yesterday morning, and winter came quickly. At 11:00 I put on my longjohns. Last night we had some light rain. This morning the ground was covered with snow. Today was windy and cold, around thirty-five degrees. I wore all my warm clothes.

We rode horseback today, sorting cattle on the alfalfa field. Then we hauled them up to some wheat pasture on the flats.

When we gathered the House Pasture this morning, I got after a silly steer. He went through the fence into the Middle Pasture. I followed him until he dived off into a deep ravine, then I gave up and left him. Later, Tom and I went back to get him. I got first shot. The steer took me and Calipso on a merry chase, up hills and down steep banks. Every time I got close to him, he dodged to the right. I didn't throw junk but waited for a decent shot. Next time I saw him cut right, I nailed him. Sure felt good.

December 2, 1980

We have moved most of the yearlings from the ranch up to stalks and wheat fields on the flats. I think we will start feeding the cows soon.

Interest rates are at eighteen percent. How can anyone make a living at that rate?

December 6, 1980

We have had a week of warm weather, which is good in some ways but hard on the cattle. They seem to tolerate extreme cold better than heat at this time of year.

We have had trouble with some young steers on the Anderson wheat. Three days ago I rode through them and cut out three sick ones. I drove them to the corral, loaded them into the trailer, and took them back to the ranch. Yesterday I found two more that were sick, and one of them was so weak that I couldn't drive him. I had to rope him and tie him down and drive the trailer right to him.

Scottie went with me yesterday and rode Lightning. I had to rope another steer and I caught him deep, around the chest. He was sick but had plenty of fight left in him, and I had trouble dragging him into the trailer. Scot got behind him with a hot shot and buzzed him until he loaded.

When I check the Anderson place, I park my trailer out in the field so that I have the option of driving sick animals to the corral or roping and loading them in the field. In some situations it is better to rope them. These steers are small, around 400 pounds, and about the right size for Calipso.

December 19, 1980

Yesterday Tom and Lawrence went to the bank to renew their loan for another six months. The day started off badly. The prime lending rate was up to twenty-one percent and around 9:00 a norther blew in, turning a golden Indian summer day into one that was foggy, windy, cold, and grim.

The session at the bank was also grim. The ranch lost money on the wheat pasture operation last winter, in spite of all the days we spent riding in rain and mud and snow, roping sick cattle, hauling hay, slogging through slop and mud. Why did we bother? We could have gone to Acapulco with two horses and ten head of roping steers, and the result would have been about the same.

The Chrysler Corporation is also having some money problems, but they are going to get a $400 million loan from the federal goverment. Last week, a baseball player signed a contract for $12 million. This economy is really screwy.

December 20, 1980

Things have been pretty grim around the ranch. Tom has been in a blue mood ever since the meeting at the bank. He thinks this might be the last roll of the dice. If we hit the market right, we might make it.

After work, we sat around Tom's woodstove and talked. I feel for the guy. I know, better than anyone, how hard he has worked for this ranch. I was beside him all those days last winter when he was so exhausted he could hardly walk.

December 21, 1980

Last week I took Calipso up to the Anderson place and checked the steers. I found a little black baldie that looked puny, so I drove him toward the trailer. When I had the right shot, I dropped my loop over his head and loaded him up.

Then I went back and checked on a nice fat Hereford steer that had been standing off to himself. He had a limp in his back leg, so I drove him to the trailer. I threw four loops into the dirt and finally caught him on the fifth.

I was so disgusted, I could have screamed. That just goes to show that you never want to brag too long or too loud about what a fine cowboy you are.

December 26, 1980

Several days ago I was given the job of checking all the cattle on the flats, about 500 head. I took Calipso in the brown trailer.

My first stop was the Weldon Wright Place where we have 104 big yearlings. As I rode out to count them, I saw a black baldie off to himself. Even a quarter-mile away, I could see that he was bloated. I rode through the rest of the steers (they were all right) and started driving the bloater toward the trailer. He was a bad case. I think he might have died within twelve hours if I hadn't found him.

As we approached the trailer, I dropped a loop on him and hauled him up to the trailer gate. I half-hitched the rope and left Calipso to hold him while I ran the rubber hose down his guzzle and let the gas escape. After I'd done this, he felt good enough to fight me when I tried to load him into the trailer. That's gratitude for you. He weighed about 600 pounds and put up a good fight. I guess my front cinch was a bit loose, because the saddle slipped up over Calipso's withers and almost to her neck. I had to take the rope off the saddle horn and tie it to the trailer.

I fought that steer for half an hour. Weldon Wright happened along at that moment and he helped me. We had to put a horse halter on the steer's head and then winch him into the trailer with fence stretchers.

The cattle on the Osborne place were all right, but on Bryan East I found a heifer with bloody scours. I drove her three-quarters of a mile to the pens. There, instead of going through the gate, she turned and ran west down the fence, back toward the other cattle. Calipso knew what to do and I nailed the heifer before she had gone twenty steps. I dragged her into the corral and loaded her into the trailer.

On the Anderson West Place, I found a steer that was gaunt, weak, and bothered with scours. I drove him toward the trailer. He ran through my first loop but I caught him on the second. From there, I drove down to the ranch, crossed the creek south of Tom's house, and checked a small bunch of cattle over on Northup Creek. This is a heavily wooded pasture, with lots of hackberry, chinaberry, native elm, and cottonwood timber.

I found a small heifer that was gaunt and poor. I drove her out of the wooded bottom and toward the trailer. At the top of the rise, she broke east and ran back toward the trees. Calipso and I went after her. She didn't give me the shot I wanted and I could see the timber up ahead. I would have only one shot and I would have to make it in a hurry. If I missed, she would lose herself in the timber. She was run-

ning to the left of us, against a barbed wire fence. I brought
up my loop, swung it twice, and threw under Calipso's neck.
It worked. When I dallied and stopped, the heifer was right
at the edge of the timber.

Useful piece of equipment, that twine.

January 6, 1981

Yesterday I checked all the cattle on the flats. I went first to
the Anderson place. Down at the ranch it was a clear sunny
day, a balmy thirty-eight or forty degrees, but up on the flats
the wind was blowing hard and it was chilly.

The Anderson place consists of a wire pen, a ten-acre
junkyard, and a field of wheat and milo stalks. The water
tank sits inside the pen and to get to water, the steers must
pass through the junkyard, which holds an assortment of
things: post piles, stacks of lumber, old farm machinery, an
old truck, and four or five old cars. The cattle often lie around
in the junkyard after they have watered, because it gives
them some protection from the wind, but it is hard to see
them there and easy to mess up a count. The first thing I did
yesterday was to ride through the junk, driving the steers
out into the open where I could see them. I counted fifty
head, counted them again, and felt that I had seen them all.

Then I rode out into the field and spent half an hour
riding through the rest of the steers. They didn't run or scat-
ter and I got a good count. But I came up one steer short,
158 instead of 159. I rode through them again and got
another count, the same: 158. Maybe one had strayed or died

in the stalks, or maybe I had missed one in the junkyard. I wanted to get a full count here because these were fresh cattle that had not straightened out, and we'd already lost two with pneumonia.

I went back to the junkyard. If I found only fifty head, I would still be short on my count. This time, I walked it afoot, checking out every hiding place. I drove the steers out into the open and counted fifty. Still one short. Then I happened to look around and saw a steer peeking out over the steering wheel of one of the wrecked cars.

He was inside the car and appeared ready to drive off.

The left door of this old Ford Mustang was missing and the steer had gotten inside. For reasons known only to the steer, he had not been able to find his way out again, and from the amount of manure on the floor and the gauntness of the steer, I figured that he had been there for two or three days.

I went over and tried to shoo him out the door. He tried to exit through the right window and windshield, and soon he had gotten his head caught between the steering wheel and the roof. Finally I got him turned around so that he could see the open door, and he scrambled out and went straight to water.

Had I not found him, he probably would have died. The stupidity of cattle should never be underestimated.

January 10, 1981

Nice weather, days up into the forties and fifties, sunny and dry. It is great weather for this time of year.

Yesterday Tom built a new roping dummy that simulates a steer running with his head down. It forces us to dip the loop, throw it open, and place it perfectly. Slop will work on some roping dummies, especially those with horns, but not on this one. A horn-roper would go crazy trying to catch this one.

After we had played on the dummy, we roped and castrated eleven bulls in the lot. Tom, Lawrence, and I had a little contest on heeling. Tom won with three catches out of five throws. I was second with four out of nine. Lawrence had four of eleven.

January 19, 1981

We cut sixty bulls the other day, part of a hundred-head shipment we got out of Arkansas. Ronnie Soviar helped, and he is a good man to have around on such occasions. He weighs 235 pounds and used to play linebacker for Georgia Tech.

It had snowed the day before and was crisp, but the sun came out and we warmed up with the work.

January 24, 1981

This warm weather continues. It was seventy in Amarillo yesterday. It's nice but we are having health problems with the Arkansas steers, and I would imagine that warm days/cold nights are part of the problem.

Thursday, Tom and I spent the day moving cattle around on the flats and roping sick ones. When we got back to the

Cutting bulls in the front lot. John on Calipso, Billy Nowlin on the tail, and Tom Ellzey on the rope.

Cutting bulls in the front lot. L–R, Jack Ellzey, Nathan Ellzey, Bill Ellzey, Billy Nowlin, John Erickson.

ranch, we had twenty-five in the sick pen. We had two deads lying in the corrals from the day before. Another had died in the sick pen during the day, and a little mutton-headed steer was staggering around in the alley, just waiting for a chance to die. It looked grim when we got there around 5:00. We had to doctor everything in the sick pen and had only one hour of daylight. We worked into the night and got it done.

February 1, 1981

Last week Tom decided it was time we got to work breaking some horses. Uncle Jack Ellzey had been working on the ground with Chief and wanted Tom to ride him.

On Wednesday we saddled him and Tom trimmed his feet. Jack snubbed him up to Babe, his mare, and led him around the corral. Tom climbed on and off several times, and then he was ready to ride him. Chief did pretty well. He bucked a few times but Jack, who is sixty-five and a retired Methodist minister, had him snubbed up close and he didn't cause much trouble. Once he lunged forward and the bit shanks hit Jack in the face. Jack is a good horse trainer and handled himself well. So did Tom. He kept his seat.

The next day, Tom decided we should go to work on Casey, a bay gelding about four years old. This horse has become a pain in the neck. He's a pushy horse and he has no respect for anyone or anything. If you try to catch him in a big lot, he'll run away from you. If you manage to sucker him into a smaller pen or a stall, he'll play ring-around-the-rosie with you or push against a gate until it pops open. He has snapped several gate chains and cracked several top boards in the corral.

Tom and I had been building up a grudge against Casey for months, and on Thursday Tom said it was time to change his attitude. The story on Casey is that he was taken to a horsebreaker at the age of two and was green-broke, but then he suffered a bad wire-cut to his foot and had to be turned out to pasture. No one has ridden him since, and he doesn't know who he is, whether he's a ranch horse or a wild mustang.

Tom managed to get a halter on him and tied the lead rope to an inner tube, which was chained to a stout corral post. When Casey went back and fought the rope, the inner tube pulled him back and allowed him to struggle without hurting himself. After he had fought the inner tube for a while, our next job was to break him to lead. I threw my saddle on Popeye, the stoutest horse on the ranch. I was uneasy about working with Casey. He's almost full-grown, a short well-muscled "bulldog" type of horse. I had broke yearling colts to lead, but I had never snubbed up a horse as big and stout as Casey.

I climbed on Popeye and began leading Casey around the front lot in the corral. He followed for a while, then decided to resist. He went back on the lead rope with all his strength. I dallied and held on. Popeye, who had held some heavy loads in his time, dropped his big Quarter Horse rump and dug in. I have never been in a situation when there was more force at work. The combined might of these two big horses was exerted on my saddlehorn, and it really spooked me. If any part of the equipment had broken under the strain—front cinch, back cinch, saddlehorn, rope, halter—it would have been a wreck.

Casey went back on the rope, threw his head, then lunged forward and went up on his back legs. Popeye was as nervous as I, and he moved away and I gave slack at the dally. I led Casey around the lot again, and he kept pulling the same stunt, lunging back on the rope and fighting. Once or twice, he caught Popeye at an angle and jerked him sideways. Pops didn't like this at all and started getting a little snorty himself. Once, when Casey went up on his back legs, I slacked the dally and sent him falling over on his side.

Tom was ready to mount up and get it over with. He climbed on and off several times, then threw his leg over and took a seat.

We were operating in a small square pen and I was nervous about what might happen. Casey still had too much fight in him and I wasn't sure what to do if he started bucking hard. If I slacked my dallies he might fall over backward, but if I held tight Popeye might jerk him down. Neither would be very good for Tom, it seemed to me.

We led him around the corral and Tom said he could feel every muscle in Casey's body. He started bucking and threw his head up into Tom's face and bloodied his lip. When he threatened to do it again, I said, "Let me take him out into the pasture and put a sweat on him."

I led him out into the Home Pasture and walked him for fifty yards. When I kicked Popeye into a trot, Casey lunged against the rope. I was caught a bit by surprise. I had the rope loose-dallied on the horn. Casey hit the rope with such force that it burned big chunks off my dally wraps and welded them onto the nylon rope. The air smelled of burned rubber, just as though someone had thrown an inner tube into a fire. I led him two circles in front of the corral and put a light sweat on him. We went back into the lot and Tom climbed on him again. He was some better this time, but when we quit, Tom and I had bad feelings. We weren't sure we were going to break this horse. He just might be too much for us—too old, too strong, too rebellious.

The next day, Friday, Tom caught Casey and tied him to the inner tube and started sacking him out with a saddle blanket. Casey went back on the rope and fought like a tiger. I was watching and said, "Hmmmm." I took off my vest and joined the party. Tom was on the left and I was on the right, and we went to work, sacking out this little smart aleck. He lunged, fought, fell down, and bucked, and the more he fought, the louder we yelled and waved.

This went on for half an hour, until Casey had begun to suspect that he was wearing himself down for nothing. He broke a sweat and finally he wouldn't booger. I led him out into the pasture and trotted him around behind Popeye. When we returned to the corral, he wore a good lather and was breathing hard. Tom stepped into the saddle and we led him around the pen. Casey was too tired to fight and we had a good session. We needed it.

Yesterday, Saturday, we hooked him up to the inner tube again and sacked him out. It was as though he had never been through this before. He went back on the rope and fought—and the halter rope broke. Zing! It went flying through the air like a bullet. If it had hit one of us in the face. . . .

We got another lead rope, hooked him to the inner tube again, sacked him out, picked up his feet, and warmed him up in the pasture. Tom got aboard and rode him around the pen. Everything was going well, so he said, "Let's go out into the pasture."

We opened the gates and went out. I was on Popeye, holding the lead rope. Outside, Casey seemed more nervous and started bucking. Tom stepped out of the saddle. Casey went back on the rope. I held my dallies and Pops squatted down against the strain. Casey leaned against the rope with all his strength, then fell over on his side—fell just like a brick wall. He got up and tried it again, but this time I'd had enough of the little snot. I turned Pop to the south, spurred him into a lope, and we jerked Casey out of his tracks and sledded him around in a big circle. Outside the small pen, I could use Popeye's strength to full advantage, and I did so with considerable glee.

Every time Casey balked, I let Pops jerk him. Pops seemed to enjoy this as much as I did, as if he'd gotten a bellyful of this rebellious little jackass. Working with Casey has confirmed something I learned several years ago up in Beaver County: never get into a fair fight with a bronc. Use every trick and advantage to break down the animal's will to fight.

February 6, 1981

We have been working with Casey for a week now and have made a lot of progress. We've worked with him an hour a

day, every day. Yesterday I took him out and led him around
to warm him up. I took him at a trot and a lope, dallied up,
and let Pops drag him when he didn't want to go at that
speed. I took him down into the sand along the creek. Then
Tom got aboard and we went out again. Casey didn't try to
buck. We worked him in the sand until he broke a sweat,
then took him to the corral and Tom practiced neck reining
in the front lot. The horse has gentled down better than we
ever expected. You can do almost anything to him now and
he will show a mild response.

He doesn't have a good whoa yet, and that is a problem.
Yesterday he was slinging his head when Tom tried to stop
him. We are using a hackamore on his head, with a steel
nose band. I think we should go to a snaffle bit.

February 7, 1981

Several days ago it was my job to feed the fifty steers in the
Home Pasture. These are new cattle that are not quite
straightened out yet, and we check them carefully every day.
I put out ten bales of alfalfa, got on Calipso, and rode out to
look them over and count them.

I was eight short so I rode down the creek looking for
them. I found them on the south side and drove them to the
feed ground. Seven went to the hay, but one, a thin red-necked
steer that had spent a lot of time in the sick pen, had
another idea. He ducked into the willows along the creek
and tried to escape. He crossed near the point where Northup

Creek joins Wolf Creek. He climbed up the other bank and went south, following Northup. I went after him. Northup is quite deep at this point and has steep banks on both sides. We have lost cattle who have fallen in or who have walked out on the ice and broken through.

I got around the steer and shoved him north, toward the others. He ran along the edge of Northup until he came to an old elm tree that had fallen into the creek. It blocked his path, but instead of going around it, he just plowed right into it. He lost his footing and tumbled off the bank onto the ice. Northup was frozen solid and had been for several months. Luckily, the ice was thick enough to support him and he skated around for a while.

I knew I had a problem here. The banks were so steep that he couldn't climb out, yet if he stayed out on the ice long enough, he would eventually step on a thin patch and fall through. I couldn't get Calipso close to the creek bank because the dead tree blocked our path. Otherwise, I would have tried to rope him and drag him out. I didn't know what to do, so I just sat there and waited.

He skated around for a while and then decided he would try to climb out the way he had come. He stumbled around in the tree branches and tried to climb up the bank. Then the ice broke, and he began slipping into deep water.

I jumped off Calipso, picked my way through the dead tree, put a loop around his neck, then threw a half-hitch around his nose. I tied my end of the rope to a big limb of the dead tree. By the time I did this, he had sunk to his neck, and my rope was all that held his head out of the water.

I jumped back on Calipso and galloped back to the corral. I had studied the problem and knew that I couldn't get the steer out by myself. He was tangled up in the tree limbs and wedged between the ice and a limb.

When I got to the corral where Tom was working with Casey, I told him to get a chain saw, all the ropes and chains he could find, and to drive the flatbed pickup over to Northup. If we didn't get the little dummy out of that frigid water, he would die or catch pneumonia.

Tom dropped everything, ran to the pickup, and drove up to the machine shed. I loped back to Northup and began clearing dead limbs away so that we could get the pickup close to the edge of the creek. Tom arrived a few minutes later and went to work with the chain saw, cutting big limbs and pushing them into the creek. I hooked three chains together, fitted one end on the hitch ball of the pickup, and wired the other end to a nylon halter. While Tom held the steer's head out of the water, I fitted the halter on his head.

Tom threw the pickup into four-wheel drive and started pulling. The steer came out of the ice and up on the bank. We turned him loose—and would you believe it? He tried to go right back into the frozen creek! I saw what he had in mind and turned him, and at last he trotted off to join his pals at the feed ground.

He was lucky to be alive. If Tom hadn't been around, if we hadn't had a chain saw handy, I could never have gotten him out by myself.

✦ ✦ ✦

We've been having a terrible time with the Arkansas steers. We've had them in and out of the sick pen, and we've lost five of them, all chronics that lingered and slowly declined, in spite of all the medicine we poured into them.

February 12, 1981

Several mornings ago, Lawrence and I hauled our horses up to the Bill Trayler wheat and rode that bunch, looking for sicks. They looked all right and we were pulling out to leave when we saw Mrs. Lewis Anderson. She waved us down and said we had a sick steer out in the Anderson stalk field. We trailered over there and found him lying down, a black baldie.

Lawrence got the trailer in position and I rode out to see if I could get the steer on his feet. He was very sick with pneumonia. I didn't think he could get up, but all at once he leaped up and started running toward the trailer. I had a loop ready and stuck it on him. I was driving him on a loose rope when he stopped suddenly. I didn't control my slack soon enough and Calipso stepped over the rope. I gave slack and tried to back her up, but the steer took off again. The rope tightened around the mare's front legs and she started bucking.

I pitched the rope away. The steer ran down a lister furrow toward the trailer. I told Lawrence I'd lost my rope, and when the steer went past, he grabbed it. I galloped forward and took it, thus saving myself some embarrassment at being disroped.

We loaded the steer. He was in bad shape, so we took him to the vet in town and got him a shot of something special in the vein.

The next day was gray and cold. At daylight the temperature was down to seven degrees and a vicious wind was howling out of the north at twenty-five to thirty-five miles per hour. It snowed off and on all day. The temperature at noon was down to five degrees and Guymon radio said the chill factor was minus thirty-seven degrees. That is killing cold. It wasn't a fit day to be out, so naturally we went out to feed cattle.

I wore my wool long johns, with six layers of clothes above the waist and three below. My outer shell was my big cowhide coat.

We drove through the steers on wheat pasture in the morning. There really wasn't much we could do but it is Lawrence's nature to get out in this kind of weather. He can't stand to sit around in a nice warm house while his cattle are out there suffering. If we couldn't make them comfortable, at least we could suffer with them. As we drove through the cattle, he shook his head. "Just look at those poor miserable things! I don't know how they can stand it. They sure need a windbreak." On the Bryan Place, we threw eight bales of feed into the hay feeder. We were out in the wind for fifteen minutes, which was enough to make my face ache.

We drove down to the ranch, fed the horses, doctored a sick steer, and chopped ice on the stock tanks, which instantly froze again. Then we loaded up with hay and went north to feed the pastures. We were short in every pasture. Those cattle didn't want to come out of the draws and ravines, where they had some protection from the bitter wind. It took us all afternoon to do a job that should have taken two hours. I don't know that we helped the cattle, but the boss felt better.

I think this was the coldest work day I can ever remember. Last night the temperature fell to seven below zero.

February 13, 1981

Warmer weather has come again. I started the day yesterday in wool long johns and had to shed them at noon. The temperature climbed up to fifty-five degrees. Only two days before, we'd had a wind chill of minus forty degrees.

February 20, 1981

We're back to spring weather, seventy-six degrees yesterday. Gorgeous.

I found a sick steer on Trayler yesterday. I got after him. There wasn't much wind but what there was bothered me. I had to wait for a good shot, then stuck it on him.

March 2, 1981

This warm weather continues. On the creek, the trees are budding out. Janet's flowers have bloomed. Flowers in March? Oh, the fools! Don't they know that this is the Panhandle?

Last Thursday, while Tom was gone for a few days, Lawrence and I fed the ranch. We came up short a cow in the West Pasture. She'd been missing for several days. Someone needed to ride out to the canyons and find her.

Then we came up one short in the Middle Pasture. Lawrence squinted his eyes and pointed to a dark spot in the distance. "There she is." It looked like a rock to me. We drove toward it. Whatever it was, it sat on the rim of a canyon. The closer we got to it, the more it resembled a rock. When we were about 100 yards from it, the rock grew a head and moved. That irritated me, since I had already expressed my opinion and had been very sure that Lawrence's eyes were playing tricks on him. We drove around and picked our way over to the edge of the canyon. It was a big black baldie cow, and when she stood up, it became apparent that she was having trouble delivering her calf. She had been there long enough to wallow out a depression in the dirt, and her bag was red and swollen. It was a good thing we'd found her.

Lawrence took me back to Headquarters. While he went on to feed the rest of the pastures, I saddled Calipso, trailered over to the West Pasture, and rode down into the canyon looking for the other cow. The task seemed impossible. There were so many places one could hide, a guy could spend all day looking.

I first checked the water tanks and the surrounding area, reasoning that she might stay close to water. She wasn't there, so I played a hunch and rode up into the north fork of the canyon, over boulders and narrow trails. I had a feeling that she might have gone up there to have her calf.

The walls of the canyon rose a hundred feet on both sides. At last I found her, near the north end of the canyon. She and her calf were fine.

I rode out of the canyon and was surprised to find that my pickup and trailer were gone. I studied the tracks and saw that someone had driven it off toward the east. Then I realized what had happened. Lawrence mentioned earlier in the day that the flatbed pickup was low on gas. He'd probably run out of gas while feeding and walked over to my rig.

I rode east out the gate and left a trail mark in the road. I gathered caliche rocks and made an arrow, pointing east. I hoped he would figure out that I had gone to find the cow with the calving problems.

In the Middle Pasture I started looking for the black baldie cow. She would be hard to find, since she was lying down near some big rocks. At last I spotted her, just where we'd left her.

I wasn't sure what condition she would be in or whether I could drive her a mile and a half to Headquarters. I got her up and started her south. She traveled well, so well that I began to doubt that she was having trouble calving. That had been Lawrence's diagnosis, but I wasn't so sure. She was a big-framed cow, in good flesh. You wouldn't expect such an animal to have trouble delivering.

I drove her through the gate into the Home Pasture and left Lawrence another trail marker, in case he tried to track me down. I pushed the cow off the caprock and on down to the creek, opened the corral gate and drove her in. Leaving Calipso in the saddle lot, I gathered up the calf-pulling equipment: chains, come-along, a bucket of warm soapy water. I ran her into an alley and put posts in front of and behind her, took off my shirt, washed my arm, and reached into her birth canal.

I felt around. I had never run into a case like this before. Instead of feeling some part of the calf—a hoof or the head— I felt some soft, slick tissue that felt like an unbroken placenta. And then I found its tail. The calf was backwards, a breech birth. This was beyond my level of competence and I didn't want to make any mistakes on Lawrence's cow. I would have to wait for him.

About half an hour later, he showed up. He hadn't seen any of the trail markers I had so carefully built for him. He pulled on a long plastic glove and reached into the cow all the way to his shoulder. Yep, it was a breech birth. He'd been right all along.

He got one of the calf's legs out and couldn't find the other. We would have to pull it out backward, and with one leg turned back. We hooked up the come-along and went to work. It was a hard pull, but the cow strained and helped, and she was big enough to let the calf pass.

Lawrence told me of some cases that had been worse. Once he had a milk cow whose calf died and began to decompose inside her. The legs pulled off and he had to remove the calf in pieces. He admitted that he threw up in the middle of the job. I almost threw up just listening.

March 3, 1981

We got a nice wet snow on Saturday. Today, Tuesday, the sun is out in a blue sky and most of the snow has melted away, leaving the ground muddy. The wheat is starting to grow, as the soil temperature warms up, and we are keeping a sharp eye out for bloat.

Last Thursday Tom and I checked the cattle on the flats and found three bloaters. I caught one with one loop and Tom one-looped both of his. This brought our two-day tally to six catches on seven loops.

We found two heifers bloated on Bryan East. We were a mile away from the trailer when we found them, and a rain storm was moving in. We didn't have time to mess around. We had no rain gear with us and we knew that if the field got muddy, we would lose the mobility of the trailer. We talked it over and decided that the quickest way to get the job done was for each of us to rope a heifer and drive her to the wire pens, where we had left the trailer. Each of us went after a heifer, and both of us caught on the first loop.

We drove them south and east on loose ropes, until we reached the point where we had left the pickup and trailer. Tom half-hitched his dally, got down, and legged his heifer to the ground. He wanted to tie her down but he hadn't brought a pigging string. I had one but neither of us was in a position to drop what we were doing to get the string to him. I had a heifer on the end of my rope and he was holding one down.

I maneuvered my heifer in his direction until I was close enough to throw him my string. He caught it and tied his heifer down, then ran and opened the trailer gate so I could drag my heifer inside. Raindrops were beginning to fall by this time and dark clouds rolled overhead. We went back for Tom's heifer. He climbed into the saddle while I untied her legs. We got her loaded and jumped into the pickup, just as the rain grew to a steady roar on the roof.

We thought we were pretty good ropers after that, but the next day I missed two easy shots at a heifer, and Tom blew his string of one-loopers and threw more loops at a steer than he cared to discuss.

In this line of work, you never get so good that you can't be humbled.

March 19, 1981

Tuesday, two days ago, we gathered up the steers on Anderson and Trayler and started to the ranch with a herd of 280 steers. Nathan, Tom, Lawrence, and I rode. It was a nice day for it.

I wore my new chaps, a pair of chinks I bought from Capriola in Elko, Nevada. I think I'm going to like them.

We got a nice rain last week. Might have broken the drought. Should start the grass.

March 22, 1981

The cattle market is lousy. Six- to seven-hundred pound steers are going for $66–70 a hundredweight. The Ellzeys have steers they would like to sell, but they may have to take them to grass.

Yesterday we had another cattle drive. This time we moved 125 big steers from the Wright place to the Bryan place, a distance of ten miles. Lawrence, Tom, Jack Ellzey and I rode, and when we drove the herd across Highway 83, Mary Frances Ellzey and Louis Bryan were there in pickups to flag down traffic. The drive took five hours. At noon, Mary Frances caught up with us. She set up a card table in the ditch and fed us a good hot meal. We ate on paper plates. Tom and I ate first, while Jack and Lawrence held the herd. Then we swapped.

The bane of this kind of drive is the kind of half-fence you find around many of the fields, one that isn't good enough to turn cattle, but which hasn't been taken down. Rusted barbed wire lurks in the weeds. We also ran into several electric fences that had not been used for years but which the owners had not rolled up. The people who leave such fences don't ride horses. If they did, they would clean up the mess. Riding a horse through such stuff is danger-ous. Calipso was nervous all day.

I rode drag most of the day and threw heel shots with my new Smith rope. It's a dandy. It holds its shape.

While we ate lunch, Mary Frances discussed a Shakes-peare play she had seen recently on PBS.

March 25, 1981

It has been a very windy month. Yesterday I fed hay in a stiff south wind. This morning my eyes burn from the wind and the alfalfa leaves. The wind has gone to the north and it is trying to rain.

Several days ago I fed the north pastures and was on my way back to Headquarters when I saw a cow off by herself in the Middle Pasture, so I drove to her. She was a small cow with big horns and I could see at a glance that she was having trouble calving. She was restless and hollow-eyed.

I went back to Headquarters, loaded Calipso in the trailer, and took all the calf-pulling equipment with me, in case I had to do the job in the pasture, although my first choice would be to load the cow in the trailer and take her down to Headquarters, where the facilities are better.

I unloaded Calipso and started driving the cow toward the Four Corners corral. She didn't want to go, so I roped her by the horns and snubbed her to the stock trailer. Then I drove an iron stake into the ground, which would give me an anchor for the block-and-tackle, if I needed to pull the calf. When I reached up into her birth canal, I found the calf alive and in good position, except that he had one front leg turned back. I got it straight and pulled him out with the block-and-tackle.

The cow fell down in the middle of the delivery. I held the calf upside down to clear its lungs of liquid, then slacked the rope so that I could take the loop off Momma's horns. As soon as I gave her slack, she jumped up and started hooking at me with her horns, which were big and sharp. She hit me on the hand and it hurt. All right, I moved the calf out of the way, so that the cow, in her stupidity, wouldn't trample it to death. I climbed on Calipso and, with my second rope, heeled the cow and dragged her down. While Calipso held the heels on a tight rope, I got down and took the first rope off her horns, then removed the second rope from her heels.

I thought I was finished then. Nice job, John.

I loaded all my tools, threw Calipso into the trailer, and started to drive away, then stopped to see what the cow was going to do. She got up and left the calf! Sometimes a cow, or most often a heifer, will do that, and sometimes they never go back to claim it.

I unloaded my mare and eased the cow back to the calf. She walked right past it. There it lay, wet and slimy, trying to stand up on its shaky legs, and the cow didn't pay it any attention.

I held her close to the calf for twenty minutes and she never showed any interest in it. I decided to take her back to Headquarters where we could keep an eye on her. I drove her a mile east to the Four Corners corral, rode the mile back to the pickup and trailer, drove to the corral, and loaded the cow into the trailer. I picked up the calf on the way home.

By the time we got to the Headquarters corrals, the cow had become so motherly that she wouldn't unload from the trailer, and when I tried to drag the calf out, she came after me with her horns.

That was my thanks, I suppose.

April 2, 1981

Yesterday we had to move 100 steers off the Bryan Place to some graze-out wheat on Price South, three-and-a-half miles south. Tom decided to drive them instead of hauling them in trailers. Lawrence, Tom, and I started them down the road. A half mile south Kim Thomas had some freshly weaned calves on some lush wheat. We expected to have some trouble if the two bunches tried to mix. We had run into trouble there on our last drive.

Kim's calves were either pure Longhorn or part Longhorn. As we approached them with our bunch, they came scampering toward us. Two vehicles were coming down the road. Instead of stopping and waiting until we passed, they drove through our herd. This is one of the hazards of driving cattle in the present day: people who have never handled cattle ahorseback and are in a hurry.

The second vehicle, a white pickup, got the steers stirred up and also cut me off so that I couldn't keep them from going to the electric fence. They never saw the fence and smashed right through it. The two bunches mixed and we had a mess on our hands.

We had to stop the drive and gather all the cattle in Kim's field, take them through a network of electric fences, and hope that the cattle wouldn't stampede and flatten all the fences. It took us two hours to get the mess straightened out, and after working around all those electric fences, Calipso was a nervous wreck.

The guy who drove that white pickup through our herd goes around town in boots and a cowboy hat. No cowboy would have driven through a herd of cattle. We cussed that guy all morning.

April 9, 1981

Last week Tom had a heavy heifer in the Headquarters corrals. She was rather small but had a big set of horns. She'd had trouble delivering her calf in the pasture, and by the time Tom found her the calf was dead inside her. Tom had to pull very hard with the block-and-tackle to get the calf out, and she was pretty badly torn up. He wanted to get her up so that she could walk to feed and water. He buzzed her with a hot shot and that didn't work, so he threw a bucket of water on her and buzzed her again. That brought her to life. The water added some zip to the hot shot.

For several days we gave her antibiotics and kept her around the corrals. She moved slowly in the back legs, grew thin and hollow-eyed. Yesterday she looked pretty rough, so Tom decided to put her in the squeeze chute and flush her out with water and Lysol. I ran her into the crowding pen, but she wouldn't go into the alley that led to the chute. I asked Tom to hand me the hot shot. I was in the crowding pen with her. He handed it to me and I buzzed her on the tail. She kicked but didn't move. I buzzed her in the flanks. In a flash, she swapped ends and came after me, hooking with those big horns. I put my arms up to protect myself. One blow caught me right in the middle of my left bicep.

She knocked me backward and threw me into the side of the calf shed. I was wearing my high-heel riding boots and twisted my ankle. Tom yelled, grabbed a post, and was coming over the fence to help me when she quit and suddenly ran into the alley.

She really beat me up, and it didn't take her long. My bicep had a dent in it where the horn hit. It didn't penetrate the skin or draw blood, but it bruised the muscle all the way to the bone. I went to bed at 9:30 with an ice pack on my arm. This morning I woke up at 4:00, hurting in several places. I can hardly straighten out my arm and can hardly walk on the twisted ankle.

I told Tom that the heifer had just been waiting for a chance to get revenge after he used that water and hot shot trick on her, only she went after the wrong guy.

My arm was red, white, and blue for days after.

April 18, 1981

One day last week, Tom and I loaded our horses and went up on the flats to doctor pinkeye. He took Bonnie, his three-year-old mare. She is still green but coming along and showing progress, but lately she has been trying to buck.

We trailered up to the Bryan Place, where we had a hundred steers on some graze-out wheat. We knew there were several bad pinkeyes that needed attention. Since I was riding a seasoned horse and Tom had Bonnie, we decided that I would catch heads and Tom would heel. I got after the first steer and caught him with a nice long throw, but he was running toward an electric fence. I didn't see the fence coming up but Calipso did. She slowed just as I was going for my dally. Since I had thrown long, I didn't have much rope left, and I lost it.

Tom fell in behind the steer, followed him around for a while and waited for his shot. Bonnie tried to buck but Tom kept her honest. When he got the shot he wanted, he threw and caught.

The next steer ran fast and dodged like a rabbit. I have never found a good response to that problem and I've never had any success roping a calf on the dodge. I made my throw to the right, thinking that he would dodge into it. He didn't. I reloaded and made the next throw too long, and missed again. Tom rode in and stuck it on him. Bonnie broke in half but Tom managed to dally and stay aboard.

I missed the next two steers. They ran about like Tony Dorsett, never two steps in the same direction. After I had run the dodges out of them, Tom caught them. On the fourth steer, just as I rode in and caught the heels, Bonnie cut loose and bucked as hard as I've ever seen her buck. Tom threw away his rope and concentrated on bronc riding. The mare bucked for thirty yards and Tom put a good ride on her.

I cheered him on, while holding the steer by the heels. When Tom got her lined out, he rode back, picked up his rope, and we finished the job.

I wasn't proud of my day's work. I missed three steers and was disarmed by the fourth. Tom had four out of four, and he did it on a bronc.

✦ ✦ ✦

We've been having some damp cloudy weather. Grass is greening up in the pastures. Cattle are getting harder to feed. Trees are leafing out.

May 7, 1981

Last week Brett Clark came for a visit from Odessa. He is twenty-two and is Tom's first cousin on his mother's side. While he was visiting, he got drafted for some ranch work.

We got a heavy rain up in the north pastures, enough to wash out the water gaps. Brett and I were assigned to put the gaps back in. We found six of them washed out. We had to strip down to our shorts and work in waist-deep water. Twelve hours after the storm, we found drifts of pea-sized hail on the bank. The water was frigid, so cold it made my legs ache.

We thought we had put in all the gaps but we missed one, between the Dutcher horse pasture and Dutcher North. Yesterday we found the Dutcher North heifers in the horse pasture, so Brett and I saddled two horses and rode over to correct the problem. Brett rode Deuce, I Calipso. I was worried that we might run into Tuerto, the one-eyed stud horse, and have some trouble, but he didn't bother us this time.

We pushed the heifers through the water gap and got down to put it back in place. I dropped the reins on Calipso, as I always do. I rarely tie her when I get down because she will stand "ground tied." Brett tied Deuce to a post and we started shaking the drift and debris off the water gap wire. Deuce, the counterfeit, cheating, low-down so-and-so, went back on the reins, broke his headstall, and galloped away. Calipso decided to go along. I had left my rope lying across the saddlehorn, and I was sure it would be lost.

We were afoot. I told Brett to finish putting in the water gap and I started walking after the horses. I hoped they might run a hundred yards and stop. I thought maybe Calipso would have enough sense to do that, but Deuce was another matter. He was, to use Tom's phrase, "a hardened criminal." He would do nothing to help a stranded cowboy. My strategy was to catch Calipso and then ride after Deuce.

I walked up the draw and found no horses. I hiked up on a ridge and looked around. Nothing. Then it occurred to me that they would have run to the corner of the pasture closest to the Headquarters corrals. I started walking in that direction, and down below me, Brett did the same. We both hiked up to the top of a rocky ridge, and there below, in the corner, were our horses. We went down to them. Deuce started to run away, the low-down #@%&*###, but we cut him off and hemmed him in the corner.

We caught Deuce first. Brett looked at the headstall and pronounced it beyond repair, but I patched it back together with baling wire and my pocket knife. Then I caught Calipso and spanked her with a stick. I dropped the reins on her and started reeling in my rope, which by some miracle had stayed on the horn. Calipso turned and ran away.

That really burned me up. I got on Deuce. The stirrups were set for Brett, who was four inches shorter than I, and I felt like a jockey in his saddle. I didn't care. I was mad and went after Calipso, building a loop in my rope. I intended to spank her all the way back to the corner and then rope her by the neck, just to let her know that a professional ranch horse *does not* leave her cowboy friends afoot in the pasture. I ran her to the corner. By that time I'd had second thoughts about roping her, and anyway she stopped. I caught her and slapped her on the legs and flank with my rope.

This was the first time she has ever quit me in the pasture, and I've left her ground tied hundreds of times. She wouldn't have done it this time if she hadn't been influenced by Deuce. I didn't want her to pick it up as a regular habit.

May 16, 1981

Last week was pretty dull—cutting cattle on the flats and shuffling them here and there; cutting out cows at the ranch, running the tractor; cutting, raking, baling, and stacking the first cutting of alfalfa; moving the irrigation pipe. But on Thursday Tom and I saddled up and went out to doctor pinkeye, and to check all the cattle. It was a gorgeous day, the kind we rarely see when we rope. No clouds, no wind, no mud or dust or snow. We had clear sky, sweet spring air, and warm seventy-degree sunshine.

I caught the first calf with lightning speed, and Tom added a perfect double-hock heel shot. I'll bet we had him bedded down in about ten seconds, which is arena-class time. But the next one humbled both of us.

This half-blind steer in the Northwest Pasture took care of Tom's perfect record the last time we roped. He dodged like a goat and several times Happy was completely faked out of his drawers. Finally Tom got tired of the chase and threw long. It didn't quite get there, so I moved in. By this time the steer wasn't dodging and I stuck a loop on his neck. Before I could feel proud of myself, the steer suddenly took off running to the right. I went for a quick dally and missed, and he took my rope away from me.

I was carrying a second rope, a little three-eighths kids' rope that I carried for just such occasions as this. Tom is the one who came up with the idea of carrying one of these. I had never been forced to use it in the pasture, but now was the time to find out how well it worked.

Tom went after the steer and threw a Hail Mary loop, but it fell short. Happy was boogering at my dragging rope and gave Tom no shot at all. I had my little rope down by then and joined the chase, rode in, got an easy shot, and laid it on him. The little rope worked fine, though I am sure it would be useless in a high wind.

We found a lot of pinkeye in this pasture and ended up roping eleven head. Tom made several long herd shots, with one twirl of his rope. He's deadly with that throw.

I made one herd shot that I was proud of. I rode into the herd, passing the steer on my right side. Then I turned in the saddle, threw behind me, and pitched a hoolihan on his neck. Tom couldn't believe it. He didn't know that I had tried that shot several days before on one of his dogs. I was out riding the Home Pasture and his dogs, Drover and Sadie, went with me. They walked along beside me until I took down my rope, and suddenly Drover slowed his pace. He was wise about the rope and knew that most cowboys can't resist roping a dog within range. That's when I tried that quick hoolihan shot, to the right and behind me, and it was the only time I ever managed to put a rope on little Drover.

Late in the afternoon, we had worked our way down to the wheat field near Cottonwood Creek. We had fifty-three heifers there. I got after a small heifer that was half blind. I was concentrating so hard on my throw that I didn't notice she was running straight toward a barbed wire fence. Lucky for me, Calipso was watching. The heifer crashed through but Calipso planted her front feet right in front of the fence and made a hard turn to the right. I lost both stirrups and almost went into the fence. I gripped the saddle swells with my legs and managed to hang on. It wasn't pretty or graceful, and it messed up my back. Five days later, I finally gave up and went to the chiropractor.

May 18, 1981

We went back yesterday to finish doctoring the heifers on the Cottonwood Creek wheat. One of them was a big red heifer that was covered with lice. At a distance, it appeared that she was black with grease, but that smudge, which covered her face and brisket, was composed of thousands upon thousands of tiny blood-sucking lice. We had doctored her a week before with some pour-on insecticide, but she needed a second dose.

She was an ugly brute, with an oversized head and eight-inch horns on a thin 600-pound frame. She looked somewhat like a buffalo. Tom caught her by the horns and I heeled her. We laid her down and poured on the dope. While we had her down, we noticed that she had pinkeye, so we put a patch on one eye. Now she looked like a pirate.

We found another heifer with bad eyes, a large slick-haired red one. She seemed restless and nervous. We eased her out of the herd, but before we could make a run at her, she went to the pasture gate and jumped it, taking the top wire out as she went.

Three heifers followed her lead, including Old Lousy.

Tom opened what was left of the gate and I galloped into the Lower Section West Pasture. I got around the heifers and stopped them. Tom joined me and we pushed them toward the gate. When they got within thirty feet of it, they turned away. The leader was the slick-haired red, who was blind in one eye, and right beside her was Old Lousy, who was also blind in one eye. The other two were not blind, only stupid, and they followed.

We held them in the corner and drove them back and forth, hoping they would see the gate and go through it. They wouldn't go. Our tempers rose. Red made a break for freedom. She cut between me and Tom and headed south. I fell in right behind her and had her roped before she even knew I was there.

Tom gave a whoop of triumph. It was more than a good shot; it was Cowboy Justice coming down like a bolt of lightning.

Tom put a double-hocker on her toes. We laid her down and doctored her eye. When we were done, we didn't take off the head rope. I dragged her through the gate and then we turned her loose.

Then we went back for the other three heifers. All we had to do was ease them through the gate. That was all, just a simple job. We'd had our fun for the day and didn't need any more. Two of the heifers trotted through the gate, but what did Old Lousy do? She plowed through another fence and trotted off in the Southeast Pasture.

And then, out of sheer . . . what? Stupidity? Meanness? Out of sheer something or other, she plowed through another fence and headed north in the Daniels' pasture.

Tom was fuming mad, and he screeched, "Rope that
_____! Don't try to drive her, don't wait, just stick it on her
before she tears down every fence on the ranch!"

I did my duty. I roped her, dallied on the run, turned
Calipso toward the gate, and gave Old Lousy a ride she won't
forget. It was fun, but we paid for it by rebuilding all the
fence she had destroyed.

May 19, 1981

One day last week Brett Clark and I drove some cows and
calves to the Four Corners corral. I was on Calipso, he on
Deuce. On the way to the pens, I was playing with my rope,
as I often do at the back of a drive. This time, instead of
heeling the calves, I roped their heads and let them run
through the loop. Just as we got to the pens, however, I caught
one and the loop pulled tight around his neck. I had to get
down and take my rope off. As I was coiling up my rope,
Calipso spooked and ran down the draw.

This annoyed me severely. Not only was this improper
behavior for a ranch horse, but I had probably brought it on
myself. The last time she did this, I spanked her with my
rope. That was a stupid thing to do. If you spank her with
your rope, then what is she likely to think the next time you
stand in front of her with a rope in your hands? I had spanked
her in anger, and anger is a poor teacher. It comes back to
haunt you. She shouldn't have run away, but I shouldn't have
given her a reason for running away.

Brett was still ahorseback so I told him to ride down the draw and bring Calipso back. I forgot that Brett was young and unaccustomed to horse psychology. He rode toward Calipso and yelled, "Whoa! Come here, mare." Naturally, she ran from his voice. He loped after her, still yelling. She ran harder than ever. He couldn't catch her, and off she went to the south end of the pasture, a mile away.

The last person I wanted to see at that moment, when I had been unhorsed and left afoot, was the boss, and of course he appeared in his pickup. I was embarrassed, but as it turned out, it was a good thing that he showed up when he did, pulling a stock trailer with a saddled horse in the back. He assessed the situation, drove to the south end, and rode Happy to where Calipso was standing. He loaded her up and brought her back to me.

I appreciated that he asked me no questions and made no comments. I wasn't in the mood to discuss it.

May 21, 1981

Several days ago we planned to round up the big steers on Price North. They weighed around 700 pounds. Lawrence had hoped to sell them off the wheat pasture around March 15, but cattle prices took a dive and the boss decided to haul them to the feedlot.

So on Wednesday morning Lawrence and I went out to Price North and built a pen out of portable corral panels. Around 8:30 Tom pulled up with three horses in the trailer.

I noticed that Calipso wasn't among them, which was odd. He came walking up to us, and there was none of the usual joking in his manner. He looked very serious for a cowboy on our outfit.

"John, Calipso got cut up pretty badly this morning. I took her to the vet and they're sewing her up."

I felt as though someone had hit me in the stomach. My first thought was, "Oh no, her legs . . . barbed wire!" Wire cuts have ruined many a good ranch horse.

"Where is she cut?" I asked.

The right side of her face. When Tom gathered the horses that morning and drove them into the back lot, one of them snapped at Calipso. She wheeled around to get away and caught her face on the tin roof of the calf shed. It left a deep gash about twelve inches long. Tom said that when he saw the gash, it almost made him sick—not just the blood and gore, but the tragedy of seeing a beautiful mare maimed in this way.

Tom put my saddle on Happy and brought him for me to use. When I went into the trailer to get him, I saw a big puddle of Calipso's clotted blood on the floor. Happy's legs and hooves were spotted with blood. It had a powerful effect on all of us, and a cloud of gloom hung over our work all morning. I tried to put on a cheerful front. I knew that Tom felt somewhat responsible for what had happened, even though he shouldn't have. Those things happen with horses.

At noon we went to the vet clinic and saw the mare. She was still woozy and her lower lip was drooping from the anesthetic, but she whinnied at us. Dr. Ernest Hardy had closed the wound with thirty-two stitches, and had done a fine job of pulling the skin together. He had left a drain tube at the bottom of the cut and it was dripping bloody serum. I felt better after seeing her. She might have a scar on the side of her face, but at least she hadn't damaged her legs. A ranch horse with damaged legs is finished.

The next morning, Tom wanted to doctor pinkeye on the Price South Place. We brought up Bonnie for him and Happy for me. I had never roped off Happy before, and he proved to be quite different from Calipso. Any horse would have been. Calipso and I had been business partners for six years. We'd ridden a thousand miles together. She knew my habits and I knew hers, and roping cattle on her was like wearing a comfortable old pair of boots.

I felt like a stranger on Happy. Where Calipso ran with a smooth long stride, Happy's stride seemed short and rough. Where Calipso glided and seldom made sudden changes in direction, Happy moved abruptly. Where Calipso put me right on top of a steer and gave me the kind of short throw I wanted, Happy held back and made me throw long.

On the first steer, I missed twice on long throws. I was just getting the feel of the horse. I caught the steer on the third loop, but Happy slowed before I could get my dally laid. I spurred him hard but lost my rope. I caught the next steer on the second loop, and one-looped the next one. I was beginning to get the feel of Hap. You had to stick a spur halfway to his heart to get him to move. If I had spurred Calipso that hard, she would have thrown me into the next county. Happy was a good horse but rough. Everything about him was rough, and his gut-wrenching stops and turns bothered my back.

That evening, I picked up Calipso at the vet clinic and took her back to the ranch. I turned her out into the horse pasture on good clean grass. After a while, she came up to the feed barn where I was working. I saw her and took some grain out and poured it into a rubber tub. She tried to bend down to it but it must have hurt her too much. She bobbed her head down but couldn't reach the grain.

I went out and scooped some of the grain and fed her out of my hands. I did this for twenty or thirty minutes, while she chewed slowly. One look at that centipede of a scar told me how sore her face must have been.

May 28, 1981

Roping off Happy did in my back. It was bothering me some before I rode him, but his rough gait finished the job. I spent Friday, Saturday, and Sunday in bed, and in considerable pain.

Day before yesterday, Calipso's cut was healing nicely. The stitches were holding and the wound was draining through the tube. The swelling had gone down. But yesterday it looked worse. Three stitches had broken and the cut oozed a thick yellowish liquid. I didn't think it was pus, but it was too thick to pass through the tube. Some swelling had returned to her jaw. I called Dr. Hardy and he wasn't pleased with the report. He told me to cut the sutures around the tube and pull it out. We did that, and also gave her a shot.

Yesterday Tom rode Casey in the pasture. He is a short, stocky bay horse with almost no withers, which means you have to keep the cinch tight all the time. The horse seems to have a lot of common sense, in spite of all the battles we went through with him. He loaded into the trailer without a fight, and Tom had very little trouble with him in the pasture.

May 30, 1981

Yesterday was the day of the LZ branding. Jeff Knighton, Scottie, and I left town at 6:00 A.M. and drove to the ranch to help Tom get things ready. Day was breaking when we got there.

John heeling on Happy at spring branding 1981.

We'd had rains during the week. The corrals were boggy, heavy dew covered the grass and the air was sweet and damp. My back, which had given me fits all week, was better.

Tom gathered the horses on Popeye. I put some medicine on Calipso's cut and turned her back out, as much as I hated to. The cut was draining and oozing fluid but seemed to be healing.

Then we started saddling horses: Cookie for Jill; Casey for John Ellzey; Happy for me; Deuce for Nathan; Popeye for Lawrence; Stormy for Jeff; Lightning for Scottie; Button for Kevin Ellzey; and Bonnie for Tom. Tom had to top out Cookie, Casey, and Bonnie. Jeff warmed up Button who, the year before, had bucked Kevin off.

Around 7:45 a line of gray clouds moved in from the north and a light mist began to fall. For a while it appeared that we might get rained out, but we decided to keep going. We found coats and vests and slickers, and at 8:00 we split the crew and rode north.

Attending the branding was a western artist from Santa Fe, Gary Nibblett. He had come to take photographs of the cattle work, to paint from later. He was a nice fellow and he showed us some samples of his work, which looked very good to me.

We had both sets of cattle in the Four Corners corral a bit after 9:00. We had some trouble getting the fire started because the wood was wet, but at last it caught and started roaring. We had five ropers for the day: Jack, Lawrence, John and Tom Ellzey, and me. Jack and Lawrence tied hard-and-fast and threw mostly hoolihans, which they do very well.

I roped off Happy. We had some big calves and I needed Hap's size and strength to drag them to the fire. He did a good job for me and cheated me out of only one dally. I was heeling well and came up with a lot of double-hocks.

Tom had a hard day. Bonnie had a hump in her back and a bad attitude all day long. She was wringing her tail and throwing her head and trying to buck with him. It put a chill on his roping. He lost some dallies when she turned wrong or started pitching. It was a frustrating day for him.

Over the years at this branding, you watch the little boys start holding down baby calves and gradually work up to bigger stock. This year Kevin and Nathan were big enough to make a difference. They and Bret Stubblefield took their lumps and did a good job. Scottie, who is six, sat on some little bitties.

It was a good branding. We had a cool morning but no rain. Everyone had a great time and nobody got hurt. No one puts on a better spring branding than the Ellzeys.

Faces from the Ellzey Ranch

(left) Lawrence and Jill Ellzey.

(above) Skip Ellzey, Lawrence's brother.

(left) Jack Ellzey, Lawrence's brother.

Scot Erickson, age 7.

Janet and Tom Ellzey.

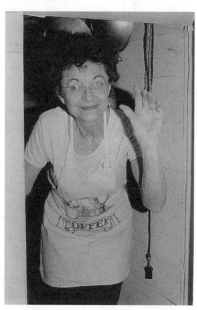

Mary Frances Ellzey.

Amy Ellzey (3) and Ashley
Erickson (2½) playing in hollow
log.

Lawrence and Mary Frances Ellzey at their roundup meal.

Kids in hay feeder watching their dads work: Amy Ellzey (4), Ashley Erickson (3), wrapped in her dad's coat, and Scot Erickson (5½), also wrapped in someone's coat.

Janet Ellzey walking past the pens with daughter Amy.

Janet holding reins while Jill pulls cholla cactus out of Happy.

Afterword

That was my last entry in the Ellzey journal. A week or so after the spring branding, I left the Ellzey ranch and went to work for Clarence Parrish as a carpenter's helper. I needed more money than I could hope to make as a cowboy, and the Ellzeys, who had taken a battering from the weather and the cattle market, didn't need the expense of another man on the payroll.

In the years since, I have continued to attend the LZ spring brandings and to help them occasionally with cattle work. As you might guess, I will always have a special bond with the Ellzey family. We have gone through much together, and they are still good people to "ride the river with."

Much has changed in the fifteen years since I left the LZ. In 1983 Lawrence made what was probably the most difficult decision of his life. He sold four sections of the ranch to Richard and Rita Sell. The combination of bad weather, a depressed cattle market, and high interest rates had left him with a debt he didn't want to carry any longer, and when the opportunity to sell the land came up, he took it.

I knew how much that country had meant to Lawrence. He had worked it, ridden it, cursed it, and loved it his whole life. He had seen his father take it through the drought of the thirties, and he had suffered with it through the drought of the fifties. But when it was time to sell, he took his bitter medicine and never looked back, never hung his head or showed any hint of self-pity. Whatever grief he felt, he kept to himself.

Tom lived for several years in the house at the Head-quarters place, running some cows and working part-time as a consulting archaeologist, the subject in which he held a masters degree. When a position opened up on the faculty at Panhandle State University in Goodwell, Oklahoma, he left the ranch and went into teaching. He and Jill still keep a small herd of cows on the Headquarters place, and Lawrence and Mary Frances still spend their summers in the house at the Lower Section.

In March of 1996, Kris and I attended a dinner party and spent the evening in the company of the Ellzey family. The occasion was Lawrence's birthday. He had just turned eighty-five. Watching Lawrence, I could hardly believe that he was carrying so many years. He is still strong, erect, and vigorous, still sings in the Methodist Church choir, still serves on the board of the Ochiltree County Hospital District, and I'll bet that he could step onto a horse and start necking calves with a hoolihan loop. When he pulled his guitar out of the case and began singing cowboy songs, my thoughts drifted back forty-five years to the time when I was a boy of seven, listening to him sing those same songs.

I was also reminded of something Mary Frances told me she thought about him when they were first married: "He has the voice of an angel and the body of Apollo." The body has paid some dues to time, but I swear, I think the man still has voice enough to outsing most of the angels.

In 1990 Kris and I bought a ranch of our own, and we're now running cattle on nine sections of rough canyon country north of the Canadian River in Roberts County, Texas. Old Calipso, my constant companion during the Ellzey years, is still with me. She's twenty-one years old now and has helped us raise and train all three of our children. It amuses me that Calipso, who was quite a hellion in her youth, is finishing out her career as a teacher. Back in our glory days, when she was bucking me off on a fairly regular basis, neither one of us would have predicted this turn of events.

I don't get too many chances to ride old Calipso any more—not because I don't want to or because she can't handle the work, but because I have to spend my time bringing along younger horses. Last summer I entered a team in a ranch rodeo put on by the Heart Ranch of Lipscomb, Texas. In front of all those cowboys, I wanted to ride my best horse, and that was Calipso. At twenty years of age, she was still the best mount on the ranch, and the best horse I'll ever ride.

I see Tom Ellzey once or twice a year, and we often remember our adventures on the ranch, the good and the bad. On cold winter days, when I look out the window and see a bitter wind driving snow straight across the prairie, I think of us riding out on Happy and Calipso, both of us

bundled up and humped over our saddlehorns, and Tom singing "Mommas, Don't Let Your Babies Grow Up To Be
Cowboys" over the howl of the wind.

Well, we *were* cowboys, pretty good ones, and we wouldn't
have traded places with anyone in the world.

John R. Erickson
M Cross Ranch
Roberts County, Texas

Glossary of Terms

bodark: bois d'arc

dally: a corruption of the Spanish term "darle vuelta," which means "give it (the rope) a turn around the saddle horn." Oldtime cowboys sometimes spoke of taking their "dolly welters." The dally method of roping requires the cowboy to wrap the home-end of his rope around the saddlehorn after he has made a catch.

four-weight cattle: those weighing between 400-500 pounds

hard-and-fast: a method of tying the home-end of the rope to the saddlehorn after catching an animal. (For a more detailed discussion of both dallying and tying hard-and-fast, see the author's book *Catch Rope: The Long Arm of the Cowboy,* University of North Texas Press, 1994.)

heeling: roping an animal's hind legs, usually after another rope has caught the head. A useful technique for capturing and containing large cattle.

Poloxolene: blocks resembling fifty-pound salt blocks but containing a chemical that helps cattle digest green wheat without getting bloated.

shrink: lose weight. Ranchers sell their cattle by the pound, so on shipping day it is important to get the cattle gathered and loaded onto trucks as soon as possible. The longer they run or stand around, the more they "shrink." In a cattle transaction involving hundreds of animals, the shrink adds up to a lot of money.

slack: looseness in the rope. Once a cowboy throws his loop and makes his catch, he must seize the rope and give it a jerk to set the loop on the animal's neck or horns. Then he must control the slack in the rope so that his horse doesn't step over it with his front legs. A dally roper will then wind the rope around his saddlehorn.

team-roping: a roping method where the cowboys work in pairs. On ranches, team-roping is used for catching and holding large cattle. One cowboy ropes the head or horns and the second moves in and ropes both hind legs. When the horses pull in opposite directions, the bovine falls to the ground. Team-roping as it is practiced in a roping arena is a sporting event recognized by the ProRodeo Cowboys Association.

waspy: nervous, aggressive, prone to fight, or hard to handle. Used to describe cattle.

Index